33
weeks of
ordinary

33

weeks of
ordinary

finding the extra in the ordinary

Brian T. Madvig

SO
GOOD
PRESS

Published by So Good Press, Wilmette, IL
For more information or to contact the author, please visit:
www.33weeksofordinary.com

hardcover ISBN: 978-0-9848316-0-9
e-book ISBN: 978-0-9848316-1-6

Jacket design by Brad Norr
Interior design by Beth Wright, Trio Bookworks
Author photo by Brad Schade, Light Design Photography

To my wife, Meg, and my children, Sam and Chloe,
who are the extra in my ordinary

and to Judy Weinstein,
who believed in this book from the beginning

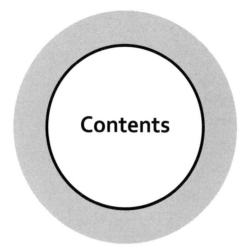

Contents

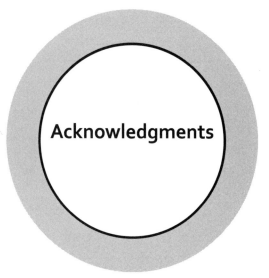

Acknowledgments

Two and a half years ago, I began feeling called to write down these stories. Some might see this calling as a midlife crisis. Some might see it as the need to further develop my right brain. I have become more comfortable seeing it as providential. Regardless of its origin, though, I am just thankful it happened.

When I looked through these stories, I was struck by how many different characters showed up. Somewhere between forty and fifty appear in these pages. Some only once, others numerous times. It reminded me how blessed I am to have great family and friends.

Thanks to Meg, my wife, and to Sam and Chloe, my children, for taking this journey with me. They have given me the time and support to make writing this book possible. I am grateful to be a part of their lives, and I love the stories we create together.

I am also grateful to my mom and dad, who brought me into their story a little over fifty years ago. Over that time we have created stories with many different flavors and tones. Through them all, I have always known they love me deeply. I appreciate my brothers and sister and their families, who have walked with me, both directly and indirectly, through many of these stories. They have been good companions.

Thanks also to all the friends I have made over the years. Some show up in these stories; some do not. Regardless, each has been a great gift to me while we have traveled through life together.

All of these folks, my family and my friends, have given my life color and depth. The result has been stories worth telling. Thanks.

A number of friends helped me get this book written. Thanks to Helen House, who coached me while I tried to figure out the next steps in my life and helped me move the book forward in its early stages. Thanks to Judy Weinstein, who encouraged me continually throughout the writing process. Thanks to Joe Higgins, Steve O'Neil, Tim Hogan, Roger Schmitt, and Paul Christmas, who read my stories, encouraged me to write more, and provided feedback as each of these stories came to be. Knowing they wanted to read my stories kept me going through many seasons. Finally, thanks to Bob Auger, who managed our private practice while I was busy writing.

I am indebted to Lance and LoAnn Peterson, who were generous in providing me a warm, quiet, and incredibly scenic place where I could get away from my usual routine to write. Thanks to Dave and Beth Peterson and Paul and Kristin Hawkinson for graciously offering me the use of their condominiums, and to Forrest and Doris Erickson for the use of their cabin at Silver Lake, so I could write for a week at a time on a number of occasions. Thanks also to Peter Hawkinson, Tom Siebrasse, and Steve Sudhoff for fostering the publication process.

This book would not be what it is without the help and vision of Beth Wallace, my development editor. Beth showed me how to create a compelling story that stands on its own, even without my lengthy explanations. If it is possible, she made editing fun. Thanks also to Beth Wright of Trio Bookworks, who copyedited the book, designed the interior, and made great suggestions while the book was getting ready to go to print. Because of both of them, this book is better than I could have imagined.

Finally, I am grateful to all of you who are reading this book. Storytellers need an audience. Thanks for being that for me.

—Brian T. Madvig
December 2011

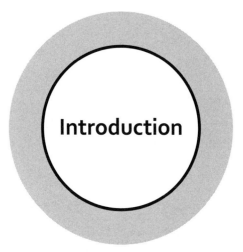

Introduction

I keep trying.

I keep trying to change the way life is. I keep trying to make it easier. I want it to be the way I thought it would be when I was growing up. When I became an adult, I would figure everything out, and things would settle into a nice, predictable routine. Nobody would be the boss of me. I'd have more fun. There'd be less pain. I wouldn't feel scared, awkward, embarrassed, or sad.

When I didn't figure out how to make my life easier in my twenties, I expected it would happen in my thirties. Nothing changed in my thirties, so I hoped I'd find a way to make it easier in my forties. I just left my forties. Thus far, I have been unsuccessful in changing the way life is. Yet I keep trying.

I keep trying because I forget.

In the Christian tradition, the church year is divided into six seasons. There are thirteen weeks of happy, pleasurable "up" time during the seasons of Advent, Christmas, and Eastertide. There are six weeks of subdued, reflective, less comfortable "down" time during Lent. The six weeks after Epiphany and the twenty-seven weeks after Pentecost are called Ordinary Time.

The church year reflects life. In most years there are about thirteen weeks of happiness and excitement; six weeks of sadness, uncertainty, and contemplation; and thirty-three weeks of ordinary when life is neither up nor down. Unlike the church year, however, in which seven weeks of Eastertide always follows six weeks of Lent, the weeks don't follow a certain order. Sometimes when I'm incredibly joyful and excited, I'm unexpectedly thrown into despair. Sometimes I experience Advent, Lent, and Ordinary Time in the same day—even the same hour. Sometimes they occur all at once. Other times, a season lasts for more than six or seven weeks. Sometimes a season can last a year or even longer.

Still, there seem to be some constants. In most weeks, life moves along with neither ups nor downs. No feeling lasts forever. I can't be excited and happy all the time, even though I might like to. And feelings like sadness and uncertainty always come, but they also always go. Eastertide always follows Lent.

I forget that life is this way, so I keep trying to change it. I'm sure I know a better way. I want more than thirteen weeks of happiness in a year. I think it will be easier if I don't have to feel discouraged anymore. I believe that if I reduced the thirty-three weeks of ordinary, life would have more zest. Then I wouldn't struggle so much.

But is that really true? Would it really be easier? Having Ordinary Time immediately following Advent and Christmas is actually a gift. When the twelve days of Christmas are over, I'm ready for a break. I love those high-energy times, but they also wear me out. The Ordinary Time allows me to catch my breath and regroup.

I wouldn't want to reduce the amount of "down" time there is in a year, either. Although I hate feeling sad or scared and lost, I know these experiences have shaped who I am. Grief has drawn me closer to others in ways I never expected.

And thirty-three weeks of ordinary is probably just about right. Ordinary has gotten a bad rap. No one wants to be ordinary. Ordinary is boring and mundane. Yet ordinary is where our gifts lie. In fact, our gifts are so much a part of our ordinary that they seem normal to us—nothing special. The reality is the more we are ourselves and embrace the way we are created, the more we use our gifts. And the more we use our gifts, the more likely we will feel fulfilled and offer something to the world. Being extraordinary means we are using extra of our ordinary.

Ordinary is also filled with wonder. I keep learning that over and over again, but I still forget. That's why I wrote this book. It's a collection of thirty-three stories that remind me that life is really quite extraordinary just the way it is, with all its different seasons. These stories are filled with laughter and happiness, but they are also filled with grief and loss. There are stories from when I was a child and stories that occurred recently. And because most of life is lived there, all these stories happened during Ordinary Time—all except for one. You'll know the outlier when you read it. These stories shaped me into the person I am today. Each has added something extra to my ordinary life.

You probably also forget that life is quite wonderful and full of joy just as it is. You keep trying to change it, too, thinking you have the ability to make it easier. You don't. Both you and I get the opportunity to laugh and cry and struggle with life just the way it is.

That's why these thirty-three stories are also my gift to you. I hope you enjoy them. In some, you will see yourself and connect immediately. Some may touch you only after a period of time. Many will remind you of your own stories, maybe even some you had forgotten. I hope you'll consider sharing those stories with a close friend, even if telling them hurts. Sharing stories eases the pain. Sharing stories also draws us closer together.

If you were thinking that these stories would be a guide for making your life easier, you're going to be disappointed. This isn't a self-help book. My ordinary gifts have never been coming up with five or six steps to a better anything. Instead, my hope is this book makes your life more enjoyable. This is a book between the self-help books. When the guidance of your most recent read no longer works, and you haven't found the next one that promises to make your life easier, these stories will be a reminder that in all facets of life—even when life isn't that easy, there really is extra in the ordinary.

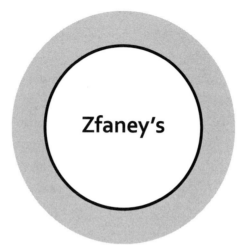

Zfaney's

One day when I was in the fifth grade, my mom served Campbell's Vegetable Beef Soup, with lima beans, for lunch. Lima beans made me gag. Unfortunately, at our house we were members of the Clean the Plate Club, and I hadn't found a good place to hide them. I told my mother I wasn't hungry.

Two hours later, I was starving. I kept watching the clock behind Mrs. Seidman's desk. Would it ever be 3:15? Inside my pocket was a shiny 50-cent piece. The night before it had been my reward for doing my chores. Today it was the solution to my hunger. Once it got to be 3:15, I was headed to Zfaney's. Zfaney's had it all: Zfaney's shelves were stocked with *Sports Illustrated*, *Popular Mechanics*, and *Car and Driver*. Zfaney's had a soda fountain where they could concoct a real chocolate phosphate or a Green River. Zfaney's had the best selection of candy in the neighborhood. At Zfaney's, a half-dollar could buy enough candy to take care of my hunger and get me a snack for later, too.

Unfortunately, when the bell rang, Mrs. Seidman didn't recognize that I was sitting straighter and quieter than anyone else, so she let Kathleen, Sonja, Gayle, and Linda go before me. Finally she picked me fifth. I jumped up from my seat and raced for the door. Mrs. Seidman yelled, "Slow down, Brian." It was clear she didn't have any idea how hungry I was. I walked a little slower until I got to the hallway. Kathleen was already gone, but I passed Sonja, Gayle, and Linda as I hurried toward the doors. Soon I was headed south down the sidewalk that would take me the three blocks to Zfaney's.

My jaw dropped when I saw that the price of candy bars had gone up a nickel, to 15 cents each. With taxes, there would be no snack for later. Before long, a Peanut M&M's, a Reese's Peanut Butter Cup, and a Hershey's Milk Chocolate with Almonds were in my hands.

I put my candy in one pocket and my change in another and headed for the door. Outside, my stomach dropped. Zfaney's only flaw was that it was smack dab in the middle of my father's path to and from work. Two hundred yards away, I spotted him. It was way earlier than usual, but my father looked to be on his way home—right past Zfaney's.

My father's voice started blaring in my head. Over and over I heard him say, "Don't buy candy. Candy is a waste of money. Use your allowance for something that matters." I didn't want to disagree with him, but those candy bars did matter.

My stomach was telling me that loud and clear. My father wouldn't get it, though. He actually liked lima beans.

All of a sudden, I thought I heard the Mission Impossible theme. I slipped undercover and stepped out of sight. With my back against the wall, I stuck one eye around the corner to see if I had been discovered. Phew! My position hadn't been compromised. My candy and I were safe—for the moment.

I cased my surroundings for a hideout. Right away I eliminated the Albany Park Branch of the Chicago Public Library. First, my father might see me as I crossed the street to get there. Second, you can't eat candy in the library. Option B was to run into the alley and hide behind Zfaney's. That plan got quickly nixed, too. The weather was hot, and Zfaney's dumpster was full. Rotting garbage does nothing to cleanse the palate when one is about to feast on nuts and chocolate.

I settled on my final option, the Amoco station across the street. On the side of the building were a bunch of parked cars. The cars would be a perfect hideout while my father passed by. My mission accepted, I peeked around the corner. My father was getting dangerously close. I sprinted the length of Zfaney's, looked both ways on Kimball Avenue, and then darted across the street. I didn't stop running until I was safely behind the second row of cars. Through the car windows, I looked for my father. He was still standing at the corner waiting for the light to turn green. *Yeah! He didn't see me!*

I leaned back against the car and began to catch my breath. I smiled. I had accomplished my mission. I had successfully evaded my father's disapproving gaze. I reached into my pocket to get my Reese's.

All of a sudden, I heard, "FREEZE!"

I looked up. What I saw almost made me fill my pants. Two cars down, the barrel of a service revolver was pointed directly at me. The policeman behind the gun was planted in a two-point stance ready to pull the trigger. Somehow, my father had called in for backup.

I raised my right hand but couldn't get my left out of my pocket. I didn't want to let go of my Reese's.

The cop saw me struggling to get my hand out and yelled, "STOP!"

I did.

"Slowly, slowly take your left hand out of your pocket."

"Yes, sir!" I blurted. "It's only a Reese's, sir."

I released my chocolate and peanut butter and raised both hands.

"Put your hands on the vehicle in front of you."

He came over and frisked me. As he was putting the handcuffs on my wrists, my father walked over to us. I was sure he was going to thank the policeman: "Thank you for apprehending my son, officer. I have told him time and again that it's a crime to waste your allowance on candy."

Instead, my father acted as if he didn't know what was happening. "Good afternoon, officer. I'm the boy's father," he said. "What's going on?"

The policeman answered, "There's been a burglary over at North Park Church. Your son meets the description of the thief. I am taking him over there to be ID'd."

Burglary? Is that all? I breathed a huge sigh of relief. Maybe my father didn't know about the candy.

Then the officer asked my father, "Would you like to ride over there with us?"

My stomach growled. I didn't want my father to come. I was hungry. He'd only postpone my feast. Nevertheless, my father nodded and climbed into the back seat next to me.

North Park Church was a block and a half away. The policeman drove the squad down the alley past the stench of Zfaney's garbage to the rear entrance of the church. The church secretary came out. She took one look at me and said, "It's not him." I felt vindicated and, if I am honest, relieved. The policeman unlocked the cuffs and let me go.

Walking home, my father asked, "Why were you down at the Amoco?"

"I was playing spy," I said. "I wanted to see if I could hide from you." I wasn't about to tell him why. I reached for my pocket to find my Peanut M&M's, my Reese's Peanut Butter Cup, and my Hershey's Milk Chocolate with Almonds. They were pretty soft, but they were safe.

Then he asked me, "By the way, what are you going to do with that allowance of yours?"

I learned an important lesson that day. The next time I had a half-dollar and Mom served lima beans, I needed to follow the sidewalk north to the 7-Eleven. Zfaney's was just too dangerous.

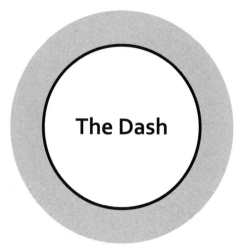

The Dash

I was one of the youngest kids in my fifth grade class, but except for a girl named Suzanna, I was the tallest. I loved to look at the class pictures. I always stood in the back row. Luckily, I was far enough away from Suzanna that the casual observer couldn't tell she was taller than I was. My height was a point of pride. Unfortunately, it didn't translate into athletic ability.

At Peterson Elementary School, athletic ability was measured by the Presidential Physical Fitness Award tests. The patches sewed on my friends' jackets flaunting their Presidential Physical Fitness Awards were a visible reminder that I wasn't fast enough or strong enough to earn one. Despite my height, the tests left me feeling very small. It was humiliating to never complete a single pull-up. It was excruciating to hang limply from a pole in front of my classmates. But running the fifty-yard dash on Christiana Avenue was even worse.

After Mr. Kaczmarek, my gym teacher, counted off seventeen cement sidewalk slabs to measure the right distance, the timed sprints would begin. Each time I ran, a puzzled look came over his face as he read the time displayed on his stopwatch. Once he even went back to his office to make sure it was working correctly.

I tried many strategies to overcome my turtle-like sprints. I tried anticipating the starter whistle. I tried leaning closer to the ground at the start. I tried shortening my stride, then lengthening my stride. Nothing worked. Even donning a pair of orange Converse Chuck Taylor All-Star High Tops didn't help. At the end of the day, all three of my fifty-yard dash attempts were the slowest in the class.

Though I was slow, I still wanted to play sports. When we moved to Minnesota just before eighth grade, I tried out for tight end. I wasn't quick enough and got cut. I tried out for the cross-country ski team as a high school sophomore. When my coach closed the race shack at a meet before I finished, I got the hint. Reluctantly I gave up on organized sports. I didn't want people to wonder if I was also slow in the head.

I never told my close friends about the race shack. I never told them I was slow. I had no desire to feel small again. Then Scott suggested we run the front gate at the Minnesota State Fair without paying. He was sure no one would ever catch us. Obviously he had never seen me run the fifty-yard dash. Had it been colder, I would have looked for the Presidential Physical Fitness Award patch on his jacket. I was about to tell Scott he was crazy when the other guys jumped on his bandwagon. They thought running the gate was a great idea. I kept my mouth shut. I wasn't going to be a killjoy.

Our creative and complicated plan could be summed up with four words: "Run for your life." The closer we got to the gate, the more I wanted to throw up. I couldn't stop thinking about the seventeen slabs of sidewalk on Christiana Avenue. There was no way this dash would be any different.

At the street corner across from the entrance to the fair, we waited for the green light to cross. We wanted to look like six of the thousands of law-abiding citizens who pay before they enter the gates. Thirty seconds later, we approached the seven arches at the entrance. To decrease our chances of being caught, we had decided to run two adjacent arches. Scott figured that with only one guard at each gate, they would be overwhelmed by six of us.

Five feet from the gate and its guards, Scott yelled, "Run!" And we were off. I heard a guard screaming "Stop." I ran as fast as I could. The screaming faded away. I didn't hear any other sounds of pursuit behind me, either. Maybe the adrenaline coursing through my blood stream was making me fast. Maybe I was going to get away.

Our plan was to run in separate directions. We'd get lost in the crowd where the guards couldn't find us. That's where our strategy failed me. My height made it next to impossible to get lost in a crowd. I couldn't believe I hadn't thought of this earlier. Before long I heard the sound of keys jangling along with the foot stomps of a guard approaching ever nearer. My legs felt like rubber. The guard screamed, "Stop!" in between panting. I could hear the anger in his voice. Evidently, I wasn't the only one who had gotten a shot of adrenaline when we jumped the gates. I dashed another fifty yards. With each stride, I was sure I was getting smaller and smaller. Then I gave up.

When he caught up, the guard clamped his hand on my arm with the strength of a vise. Between breaths, he panted, "You're coming with me."

Bent over and holding my knees, I asked for a moment. "I'm not going anywhere," I promised the guard.

He maintained his grip and waited, pulling out his walkie-talkie to make a call.

I swore under my breath. Once again I was the slowest. Once again I was at the end of the line. Once again there was no Presidential Physical Fitness Award for me. Even worse, though, the humiliation I left back on Christiana Avenue had returned. My friends were going to know I was no athlete. I felt as if I was back in the gym hanging from the pull-up pole.

A white Chevrolet Suburban with tinted windows and the word "Security" on the side drove up a minute later. The guard opened the back door and told me, "Get in." I wasn't alone. To my surprise and delight, already sitting in the back seat trying to keep a smirk off his face was one of my buddies, Merc. Merc, the captain of the cross-country team. Merc, the track sprinter.

Like Merc, I worked hard to keep the smirk off my face. I was so happy. Merc got caught too. I wasn't alone. I didn't have to explain why I was the only one caught. I could just enjoy getting into trouble with my friend. Nothing they could do to me now could make me feel like a loser. Quietly Merc and I gave each other a high five below the guard's sight in the rear view mirror.

We sat in the back seat of the Suburban for the next five minutes. My knees pushed against the driver's seat. I didn't feel small any longer. Then the driver climbed in and drove us to the front entrance. A guard opened the back door, motioned for us to get out, and sternly lectured us for ten minutes. When he ran out of things to say, he told us to leave and never come back.

Merc and I silently walked away as fast as we could. When the entrance and the guards were out of sight, we turned and gave each other a huge high five. Then we talked about how we could finally breathe, grateful that jail was not in our near future.

On the other side of the fairgrounds, Merc quietly found a secluded place to jump the fence. I had had enough excitement for the day, so I paid the admission fee and entered the nearby gate. Merc was waiting for me at the next corner, scoping out the nearest Pronto Pup stand. Corn dogs never tasted better.

.

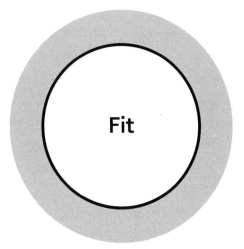

Fit

"Not again!"

A laundry basket of hand-me-downs had just arrived in my room. Mom was cleaning closets. Over the summer my older brother Bruce had grown four inches. His clothes still had wear in them, though. The fourth of five boys, I rarely got new clothing except for the Sears briefs and tube socks that filled my Christmas stocking.

Each time a basket arrived, I tore through the pile looking for the clothes I had coveted while my brother wore them. One time I discovered a Flipside T-shirt, advertising the record store where I had bought my first album: *Harvest* by Neil Young. I loved the T-shirt's white-on-black print. Another time, I got a pair of jeans faded nearly white but without holes in the knees. I got some "cool pants" comments from my friends when I wore them. Too bad they disintegrated in the dryer three washes later.

This time the basket was disappointing. Plain white T-shirts, plaid school shirts, a pair of blue dress pants, and an old swimsuit. None of them said, "Wear me. You'll be cool." I was just about to give up hope. Then I saw that underneath the layers of letdown lay a gray sweatshirt. Could it be the hoodie? The hoodie from North Park College? The hoodie that Bruce never let me wear, even when I begged?

Yes! And it was still in great shape. Two drawstring ends dangled from the hood. Both ends still had knots. The letters *NPC* were emblazoned across the front. Below the letters a pocket promised to warm my hands in the cold. The sweatshirt looked cool when Bruce wore it. Now I was going to look cool, too. I ripped off my plain sweatshirt and threw it on the floor. I shoved an arm into each sleeve of the coveted hoodie and pulled it over my head. I ran to the bathroom mirror to see how I looked in my new used sweatshirt.

"Not again!"

Reflected in the mirror stood a boy wearing a long-sleeved hoodie. Unfortunately, the long sleeves ended in the middle of his forearms.

This wasn't the first time. I can't remember ever having any sweatshirts with long enough sleeves as a kid. Even when I outgrew Bruce and his hand-me-downs, the new sweatshirts Mom bought me covered my wrists only until the first time through the dryer. I learned to push up my sleeves, acting like that was cool. Inside, I wished for shorter arms. Then the clothes would fit.

Sweatshirts weren't the only problem. Size thirteen-and-a-half feet meant that shoes were rarely in stock. Converse Chuck Taylors, the only ones that truly ran big, became my shoes of choice. "One-size-fits-all" hats should have included the phrase "except Brian Madvig." I gave up the dream of wearing a baseball cap early on. By the time the summer of 1986 rolled around, I knew what fit and what didn't. Hooded sweatshirts, like all the fun stuff, were never a part of my wardrobe.

One day that summer, my wife, Meg, and I took a day trip to South Bend, Indiana. We enjoyed a wonderful lunch in the sunroom at the old Studebaker mansion. Afterward, we drove over to Notre Dame to burn off a few calories and explore a campus we had never seen.

Soon we were walking past the golden dome of the administration building and into the grandeur of the Church of the Sacred Heart. The massive arches and deep blue frescoes inside were breathtaking. Afterward we knelt for prayer down at the Grotto with all its flickering candles.

Next we found ourselves at the House That Rockne Built, Notre Dame Stadium. I didn't grow up a college football fan. In fact, I didn't follow college football at all. My allegiance was to professional football. Still, I could hear the crowd roar after Joe Montana threw one more touchdown pass to orchestrate another of his many come-from-behind victories.

On the way back to the car, we stopped in the university bookstore. I had never seen so much green. Notre Dame paraphernalia was everywhere. Books about the Four Horsemen sat on shelves next to blue-and-gold foam footballs. There were racks full of caps embroidered with *ND*. T-shirts with ironed-on leprechauns filled table after table. Within five minutes, my eyes were spinning.

We were making our way toward the exit when I yelled to Meg, "Stop!"

"What is it?" she asked.

I pointed. Meg looked, but her quizzical expression told me she didn't understand.

"XXL! It says XXL!"

I was pointing to a tag on a beautiful white hoodie in front of me. Two drawstring ends dangled from the hood. Both ends had knots. The words "Notre Dame" were emblazoned across the front. Below the words a pocket promised to warm my hands in the cold. This one, though, had "XXL" written on a tag at the end of one sleeve.

Should I get excited? Or was the sweatshirt just a cruel trick, like Bruce's hand-me-downs and the new sweatshirts that shrank in the first wash? But that "XXL" tag tantalized me with the thought of warm arms all the way to my wrist. No sweatshirt had ever said that to me before. I couldn't resist.

I unzipped my jacket and threw it on the floor. Meg rolled her eyes and picked it up. Then I took the white hoodie off the rack and removed the hanger. Shoving an arm into each sleeve, I pulled it over my head. I didn't have to look in the mirror. This time, the sleeves covered my forearms—my wrists—the palms of my hands. All I could see was my fingers.

I began to jump up and down, beaming. I didn't want to take it off, so I walked up to the checkout and paid for it right there. The cashier cut the tags off my long sleeve, and I wore it home. I wore the sweatshirt so often that summer, someone asked if it had been sewn onto me. He didn't understand. For the first time in my life, the sweatshirt fit. Someone had made a piece of clothing with me in mind.

That day, I became a Notre Dame football fan for life.

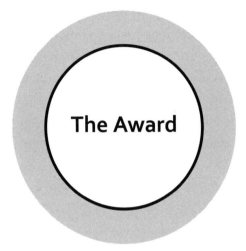

The Award

The summer after my junior year in high school, I spent a month on work crew at a camp in Colorado. Delighted to be accepted and enthusiastic about the camp, I couldn't wait for July to arrive. When Tom, the work crew director, handed out our positions for the month, I couldn't believe my luck. Rather than serving on the food line or some other boring job inside where I'd be required to wash my hands every ten minutes and wear silly-looking paper hats, I was on Specialty Crew. Specialty Crew got to dig holes in the dirt outside in the middle of the mountains. Specialty Crew got to ride in trucks. Specialty Crew was cool.

I liked the guys who were in charge of Specialty Crew, too. Bruce, the camp manager, was hearty, broad-shouldered, and sported a thick black moustache. Someone said he drove a diesel, four-wheeler pickup truck. Mark, our Specialty Crew leader, was boyish and warm, and he clearly made friends easily. His wife was expecting triplets near the end of the summer, and he laughed when we started to tease him about how busy he would be. Bruce was cool, but I wanted to be Mark's friend.

Mark's assistant didn't say a whole lot that first day. Shorter and stockier, Stew wore a stocking cap to keep his bushy hair from flying all over the place. When I caught his eye, his lips curled up into a smile, but he quickly looked away. His face remained blank when we teased Mark about fathering triplets. I hoped Stew would warm up. Otherwise, I'd find a way to avoid working next to him.

At five o'clock the next morning, Tom and Stew met us at breakfast. Still rubbing the sleep out of my eyes, I woke right up when Tom told us that during the night, Mark had received an emergency call informing him that his triplets were arriving two months ahead of schedule. He was already gone.

I was crushed. Mark and I were going to laugh and joke while the hard work of Specialty Crew put blisters on our hands. Now that dream was gone. Unexpectedly, Stew was in charge. Would we still have fun without Mark?

Our first task was to repair a wooden shed at the corral. After I had nailed my fourth board into place, Stew was still on his first. He bent one nail, then another. Then he smashed his own nail, swearing quietly as he shook his thumb up and down. At that moment, whether or not we were going to have fun ceased to matter. I saw that I could help.

With each new task we were given, I scoped out what it needed. I told Stew how it could be done well. If, in the middle of a task, I saw a way to take less time or make it better, I suggested it. Sometimes Stew followed my suggestions, sometimes not. I asked him why. He gave me vague answers that didn't really satisfy. Nevertheless, the other guys on Specialty Crew kept thanking me for my ideas, so I kept offering them.

During our second week, Bruce loaded us up into a big white dump truck with a five-speed manual transmission. As we headed into the valley to bale hay, he told us a joke about a guy on a tightrope. *This day is going to be fun*, I said to myself. Specialty Crew quickly got into a rhythm, and before long the truck was loaded. Bruce drove out of the field slowly and carefully, taking his time. One turn too quick or one start too jerky, and the bales, precariously stacked three higher than the sidewalls, would topple. Three slow miles later, we stacked the hay in the barn. Then we returned to the field to load once again. At the end of the day, I was ready to drop. What got me through dinner was the high five I got from Bruce. He loved how much hay we had stacked in the barn.

On the second day of baling, Bruce couldn't join us. I grimaced as Stew got behind the wheel. Stew had been introduced to his first manual transmission the night before. It didn't surprise me when it took ten minutes to get the truck moving. It didn't surprise me when our trip down the mountain took half an hour longer than it had the day before.

Though I only had a learner's permit, I knew how to drive a stick shift. The previous spring, my sister had taught me how to let out the clutch in her three-on-a-tree Mercury Comet. I could even start from a stop on an uphill incline without killing the engine. I knew I could help, but I wasn't sure I wanted to offer. I was never sure how Stew would respond. I kept quiet.

At the field, Stew drove up and down the rows to pick up the bales strewn about. He killed the engine over and over again. With each jerk, bales of hale tumbled off the truck. Eventually we started stacking them only one bale above the sidewalls. I wasn't sure how long I could keep quiet. Haying was getting to be a chore, rather than the fun it had been the previous day.

The morning passed. At noon the truck was only half full. I hadn't heard laughter for an hour and a half. I couldn't stand the tension any longer and approached Stew. I told him I knew how to drive stick. Since I didn't have a license, I offered to drive only in the field and not on the roads. I felt my back tighten when Stew refused. I returned to throwing bales. *Why won't he let me help him?* I thought. When we finally finished loading, Stew drove to the barn. Thank goodness there was only one stop sign on the way. We only had to restack toppled bales once.

Back at camp at the end of the day, Bruce asked how the day had gone. Stew said, "Fine," and left. I remained behind with Bruce and told him about the day. I worried he might think we had been slacking off. Bruce looked concerned, but his eyes lit up when I told him I could drive stick. I made sure to mention I only had a permit. Bruce looked away for a moment. When he looked at me again, he said, "Thanks, Brian. I'll talk to Stew about it."

The next morning, Bruce told us that Stew and he had agreed that I was going to drive the truck not only in the field but on the highway as well. *Finally, you're going to let me help you,* I thought. I looked over at Stew, wanting to catch his eye and say thanks. He didn't see my appreciation, however. His eyes were focused on his shoes.

As I drove to the field, Stew sat in the cab next to me. No words were exchanged. I felt uncomfortable, unsure why he was silent. I chose to ignore it. After all, with me driving we were going to accomplish a lot that day. Later, as the sun approached the horizon, Specialty Crew finished stacking the last of the bales in the barn. Bruce met us as I drove back into camp and asked how the day went. Stew said, "Okay." When Bruce looked my way, I smiled and gave him the thumbs up.

As the month went on, Specialty Crew built a fence around the sewage pond, filled ruts on the gravel road, and painted the dining hall. With each task, I suggested ideas for doing it the best way possible. When Stew didn't do what I suggested, I no longer asked why. I couldn't read Stew, but I knew how my Specialty Crew mates felt. They kept thanking me for making the hard work easier.

On the last night, the camp threw a party to thank us, stuffing us with a feast: salad, potatoes, baby back ribs, and flaming baked Alaska. As I loosened my belt, I thought about the month. What a great time. I had used my gifts well in the service of Specialty Crew and the camp. Though he was difficult to read, I had gone out of my way to help Stew, who clearly hadn't been ready to take over Specialty Crew. Knowing I had done a good job, I couldn't wait for the upcoming awards ceremony. Everyone got an award. I figured mine would somehow recognize those contributions.

Soon Tom and Stew began doling out the awards. Many were humorous. Sue won the award for breaking the most plates. Everyone laughed, remembering the sound of crashing china regularly emanating from the kitchen. The award for most times late to breakfast went to Rick. Best Sense of Humor went to Aaron. Sandy won Funniest Laugh.

Other awards were more serious. Hardest Working was one of those. I figured that might be for me until Mike, a friend from Specialty Crew, heard his named called. I began to get a little anxious. The ceremony was nearing its end, and the awards that seemed to fit me were already awarded. I wondered how they were going to recognize me.

The next award included the name of a guy from my cabin: John Q. When I heard the behavior it acknowledged, I began chuckling to myself. Good-naturedly we had been teasing John all month that it was one of his gifts to the world. When we teased him, he would laugh with us. I thought this award continued that teasing and looked around for John. I was sure he would be the awardee.

With a huge smile on his face, Stew announced the winner. Surprisingly, I didn't hear John's name. I didn't hear the name Stew read either. Stew repeated it again, "The winner of the John Q. Complaint Award for the person who complained the most is Brian Madvig." It was only then that my mind registered the name he announced: Brian Madvig. Me. The award was for me.

Stunned, I walked up to the front. Stew grinned and giggled as he shook my hand and gave me my award. Somehow I found my way back to my seat. There I looked at it: the John Q. Complaint Award for the person who complained the most. I was the winner? I complained the most? Me? I figured out how we could do the best job possible. I helped Stew when he needed it. I was an asset to Specialty Crew.

I had never seen Stew grin like that before, much less giggle. Why was he having so much fun? Was it because I deserved this award? Deep down, I knew he had to be right. He was my leader at a camp run by a great organization. He was the adult in charge. If he gave this award to me, then I deserved it. I had screwed up. Feeling a deep sense of shame, I wondered how I could have done such a poor job.

After the last few awards were presented, the party continued with music and dancing. I tried to look happy. I tried to dance. I couldn't. For me, the party was over the moment I received that award.

When I got home, I told everyone how the blisters on my hands burned only the first week. I told everyone the countless ways I held my nose while building a fence around the sewage pond. I told everyone I got to drive a dump truck. I never mentioned the award. I kept that to myself.

The Fury III

It was probably the most familiar, most common, most repeated litany during our high school years. Sometimes we'd repeat it for forty-five minutes to an hour. Sometimes an entire evening. That February Saturday afternoon, sitting in Steve's kitchen was no different. Steve and I were rubbing our stomachs after a tasty meal of hot dogs and sour cream and onion chips when the litany started once more:

"So what do you wanna do now?"

"I dunno. What do you wanna do?"

"I dunno."

The idea of repeating the litany for the afternoon made my full stomach start to grumble.

"How about a movie?"

"Nah. Nothing good showing."

"Skiing?"

"Nah, too late to start."

"Bowling?"

"Nah."

Then I had a moment of inspiration.

"We could try and fix the door."

"What door?"

"What do you mean, 'What door?' The door on the Fury III!"

The Fury III was Steve's ten-year-old 1967 two-toned— black on the top, Fury Red on the bottom—four-door Plymouth sedan. His parents let him drive it at the age of sixteen. They were confident not because he was a good driver, but because the Fury III was a battleship. The bench seats were so wide, it could ferry a boatload of us to our many adventures. We drove it to Mounds View High School football games. We drove it to Met Stadium to tailgate at Minnesota Kicks soccer games. We drove it to the Rose Drive-In to pick up chicks. Well, at least to try anyway.

For the past two months, though, Steve had been motoring around with the front passenger door partly open. It was partly open because Merc had forgotten to close the door while he directed Steve out of Coach's snowbank-lined driveway. The door got bent in the snowbank, and now it wouldn't close. To keep it from flying open, Steve had tied a piece of rope between the door and the steering column.

Whenever Steve climbed into the Fury III and looked over at the passenger door, he grumbled and swore. He hated that his Fury III was wounded.

"Do you think it can be fixed?"

"I dunno. But at least we can try."

"Okay, let's do it."

As we headed to Steve's garage to gather some tools, the phone rang. It was Laura, Steve's girlfriend. Steve told her we were going to fix the Fury III at his father's warehouse. I could tell she was disappointed. It was obvious she wanted to spend some time with him. All of a sudden, Steve's eyes lit up.

"Do you have a friend?" Steve listened to her response. Straight faced, he asked, "Is she good looking? Ask her if she wants to come with."

Steve hung up the phone with a smirk on his face.

"Says she has a cousin. She's pretty and lives nearby. Laura's calling her. If this works out, Moose, you owe me."

Things were happening so quickly. I wasn't sure what to think. What did it mean that they were going to join us? Were they going to help? Was this a date? Then I thought, *she might be good looking, but what if she doesn't think I am?* This might be a long afternoon.

I kept my thoughts to myself and smiled back. "Sounds great!"

Laura called a few minutes later. Larissa was game to join us. Steve and I finished loading the tools in the trunk. Twenty minutes later, Laura and Larissa were riding in the back seat. Larissa was shy but nice, and Laura was right—she was pretty. I couldn't wipe the smirk off my face. We were on our way to a warehouse to fix the Fury III. Somehow, it had turned into what looked like a date.

Inside the warehouse, I began loosening bolts to remove the passenger door. The girls sat on some boxes nearby talking to each other. It seemed as if they were in a world totally separate from me and Steve.

When we got the first hinge off, we discovered that it was made of thick steel. Bending them was not going to be easy. We placed each on a vise and hammered. Nothing happened. Then we tried a sledge. Maybe the hinges bent a little, but not much. Steve's swearing started to heat up. I wished we could use some of that heat to soften the steel.

Our frustration increased; Laura and Larissa watched. I was sure Larissa wasn't having any fun. She was yawning more often. I imagined her conversation at school on Monday morning:

"So what'd you do this weekend?"

"Watched some boys hammer hinges."

"Wow! Sounds like fun."

"Sort of."

When I told Steve about the imagined conversation, he growled back, "I told Laura we were going to work on the car."

I felt a little better.

We gave up trying to bend the hinges any farther and began reattaching the door. We hoped we had bent them enough that the door would close. When the last bolt was tightened, Steve pushed the door to close it. It bounced right back at him. He growled. With more force, he slammed it again. Once more the door bounced back. Swear words echoed off the walls.

Hope was gone. The door wasn't fixed. The swearing and our disappointment weren't creating a dating atmosphere, either. This date was turning out to be no date at all.

We retied the door and loaded the tools in the trunk. Steve backed the car out and then walked back to reset the warehouse alarm. He motioned for us to get in the Fury III but pushed me away when I tried to climb in the front seat. Then he let Laura in next to him, while he gave me a wink.

I fumbled for the backdoor handle. Evidently his wink meant the backseat was for Larissa and me. Actually for Larissa, me, and the black-and-white, twelve-inch TV that Steve had taken out of the trunk to make room for all the tools. Larissa sat flanked on either side by me and the TV. I had only known Larissa for a few hours. Now I was sitting in the backseat with her. I tried to say something clever. "That's a neat black-and-white TV" was all I came up with.

Fortunately, Larissa took over the conversation. She talked about the trophy she and her pom squad won performing her favorite dance routine. She talked about the time she wiped out skiing. It was really cold when the snow got shoved up her back during the spill. Then she asked me about the play I had just auditioned for. I began to breathe easier. Our conversation was making up for the forgettable time I had already shown her. While I was sure we were no longer on a date, at least her Monday morning conversation might not be so bad.

When Steve slowed down and took a right turn down Old Snelling Road, I asked from the back seat, "Where are you going?"

Coyly he responded, "Oh, I don't know."

When the road dead-ended, Steve parked the Fury III and switched off the ignition. "Golly," he said. "I guess it's going to get cold in here now that the engine's off. You two better snuggle up." Then he gave me another wink and started kissing Laura.

What was he thinking? Didn't he know I had already blown it? Why would Larissa kiss me when the good time I had shown her was watching me try to fix a car? It wasn't going to happen. Nevertheless, I put a smile on my face and raised my eyes to look at Larissa. She was smiling back. Then she reached up and kissed me. She kissed me! Of course, I kissed back. And then kissed back some more.

Unbelievable! Inside I couldn't stop smiling. There was no way I could have imagined this happening when I had answered Steve's question, "So what do you wanna do now?" with "We could try and fix the door." Yet here I was in the back seat of the Fury III, with a TV, making out with a pretty girl. A pretty girl I had just met. A pretty girl I had taken to a warehouse to fix a car. It was unexpected. It was delicious. It was the stuff of which adolescent dreams are made.

A half hour later, Steve fired up the engine. After he waited for the windows to defrost, he put the Fury III into gear and drove the girls home. As Larissa climbed out, I smiled and thanked her for the afternoon. With a sparkle in her eye, she smiled back and said, "You're welcome."

I climbed through Steve's door over to the passenger seat, and we drove away. Even the cold breeze blowing through the passenger door couldn't cool me off.

Steve looked at me. "You owe me, Moose," he said.

I grinned. He was right.

Two minutes later he looked at me again.

"So what do you wanna do now?"

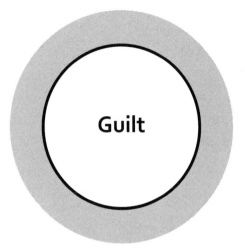

Guilt

Peter, why aren't you stopping? I said to myself.

Rain lashed at the windows. The wipers were useless. I couldn't see more than twenty yards in front of the van. Peter was driving. In the seats behind us, twelve members of our high school youth group were wrestling and laughing with each other, oblivious to the danger.

Peter, don't you know I'm responsible for their safety?

The air conditioned defroster was on high, but the windshield kept fogging. With one hand, Peter wiped and rewiped the glass with one McDonald's napkin after another. He drove with the other. My fingers dug into the armrests.

"Peter, I think we need to pull over to the side of the road," I finally said out loud.

Peter kept driving. He must not have heard me.

A little louder I said, "Peter, please pull the van over to the side of the road. It's not safe."

He nodded. And kept driving. A second later, he swerved when the wheels got too close to the edge of the road.

"Peter, stop the van now!" I screamed at the top of my lungs.

This time he pulled over. I slumped into my seat, relieved that we were off the winding mountain road at last. At the same time, a knot of guilt began in my gut. I'd just yelled at Peter. This was Peter's first trip with the youth group. In the fall, he was taking over as the youth minister. I worried that he would feel embarrassed being yelled at in front of the kids. Maybe I had hurt his feelings. Maybe he was mad at me.

When the rains lightened, I told Peter we could go. He drove in silence the rest of the way to the school where we were staying. When Peter was unloading the trailer, he grabbed a couple of suitcases and started walking in my direction. I hurried around a corner before he saw me. I didn't know what to say. I didn't feel bad about asking him to stop. I only felt guilty about yelling at him.

Throughout the week, we worked on separate work crews. We nodded at each other when the larger group got together, but I avoided catching his eye otherwise. I chose to ignore what had happened. After all, when we got back from the trip, our paths wouldn't cross. I was leaving for graduate school.

Eleven years later, Peter was called to be the associate pastor at my church. Unfortunately, time hadn't eased my guilt. Though he was cordial with me, I was sure he was still mad at me for yelling at him in the van. After all, I had humiliated him in front of the high school kids for whom he was soon going to be youth minister. I tried to ignore the guilt, but it wouldn't go away. And then our families started spending a lot of time together. His oldest daughter and my daughter, Chloe, were becoming close friends. I couldn't get away.

Eventually I couldn't handle it anymore. We were having lunch when I got up the courage to say something. "Peter, I wanted to talk to you. Something's been really bugging me."

"What's that?" he asked.

"Do you remember when we were going down through the Appalachian mountains for the mission project and I yelled at you?"

Peter responded, "You did what?"

"You remember. That huge rainstorm? You were driving the van, and I wanted you to pull over to the side of the road. You didn't, so I finally screamed at you to pull over. I've been feeling guilty about hurting your feelings that way ever since it happened. I'm sorry."

"You yelled at me?" he asked.

"You don't remember?"

"No."

"You don't remember me screaming at you?"

"No, I don't remember that at all," Peter responded.

I started to laugh. For eleven years, I had been harboring guilt, worried that my yelling had caused a rift between us. The rift was only in my mind. That day I made a commitment not to wait eleven years the next time to tell him that something was bugging me. It has served us well.

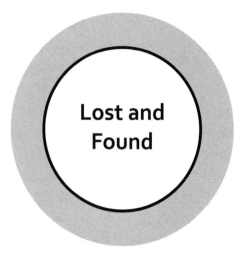

Lost and Found

The morning my sister-in-law Tina went into labor, my brother Paul called to tell me they were on their way to the hospital. It was their first child, and I could hear the excitement in his voice. I told him my prayers were with all of them and hung up the phone. I tried to return to reading Dietrich Bonhoeffer's *Life Together*, but I kept thinking about how I could join in their excitement. That's when I remembered I had credentials.

I was serving as a youth minister at the time. The requisite license gave me credentials that allowed me access to patients in the hospital. I closed my book and jumped in my car. I was about to become Paul and Tina's pastor.

When I arrived on the obstetrics floor, the nurse pointed me down the hall. Paul opened Tina's door with a sparkle in his eye. "Tina's progressing pretty well."

"Great!" I said. I wasn't sure what else to say as the pastor. I also wasn't sure I wanted any more details.

Then Paul said, "Thanks for coming. I really need to get back to Tina."

I gave Paul a big hug. "Meg and I can't wait to meet our new niece or nephew."

He smiled and closed the door. As I pressed the down button for the elevator, I couldn't stop smiling. A wonderful adventure was about to begin for my brother and sister-in-law.

Ten hours later, the phone rang again. I jumped up from the couch and answered. The excitement was gone from Paul's voice. Rebecca, his newborn daughter, my niece, had been airlifted to Prentice Children's Hospital. Deprived of oxygen during her last twenty minutes in the birth canal, she was struggling to survive. Meg and I got downtown as fast as we could. For the next few days, we basically lived in the hospital, getting to know Rebecca while she was on life support in the neonatal intensive care unit. Four days after her birth, she died.

I helped Paul and Tina prepare Rebecca's funeral. After all, I had credentials. When she had been laid in the ground, I put away my credentials and began to feel. I was angry. A week and a half earlier, Rebecca had been healthy, snuggling in her mother's womb. Now she was gone.

I wondered where God was.

Two years later, during the first week of January, Meg got a call from her sister, Beth. Meg's ninety-two-year-old Grandma Ruth had passed away the night before. Three weeks later, Beth called again. Meg's Uncle Wally had collapsed while getting dressed. A blood clot had taken him at the age of sixty. Meg screamed, "No," and dropped to the floor in tears. I joined her. Wally was our favorite uncle. Warm, friendly, and funny, he was full of life. Wally dressed up as an old Swede at our wedding and told the corniest jokes. You couldn't help but laugh, though, because it was Wally telling them. We couldn't afford to go home for either funeral. I felt incredibly isolated and alone.

Three months after that, the phone woke us from a deep sleep. It was Beth. Again. Woody, Meg's thirty-three-year-old brother, had been discovered unresponsive in his car. He was pronounced dead at the hospital. While Woody had lived hard, we had never expected him to die. This time we flew to Chicago for the funeral.

If I was angry after Rebecca's death, I was livid now. In the space of three months, we had lost three family members. I had grown up with what I thought was a gracious, loving God. What was happening to my family was neither gracious nor loving. Was this a God I wanted to worship?

The following fall, my brother Bruce experienced some baffling health problems. His doctors diagnosed a rare form of cancer. Bruce died the next June. Like Woody, he was thirty-three.

By this time, I was way past livid. I played loud, angry music as I drove to classes. I couldn't stop swearing. Where was God? Why wasn't God saving my family members? Did God really exist? I saw no evidence to support it.

Meg and I had chosen to wait to have children until I approached the end of graduate school. When I completed my coursework, we began trying to get pregnant. With excitement and anticipation, every four weeks we looked for evidence of pregnancy. Each time we were disappointed and began waiting another month. I kept reassuring Meg that it would happen soon. Silently, I began to worry.

A year passed, and we went to the doctor. The doctor informed us that my sperm had poor morphology and poor motility. He said it was unlikely we'd have children. Then he left the examination room before we could ask any questions. The nurse came in five minutes later to tell us our appointment was over.

Meg and I were devastated. I had never considered the possibility that we might not be able to have children. Was this really happening to us? First we had lost a niece, an uncle, and two brothers, all before their time. Now we were being denied children, the signs of hope and new life. For me, it was one more piece of evidence against God. I began to give up my own hope.

Yet I couldn't admit I didn't believe anymore. I was too afraid. It wasn't that I was afraid of God. God was already gone. No, I was terrified of losing Meg. She had been my only steady source of love through all of this. If I told her I didn't believe in God, I worried that she would stop loving me. Then I would be totally alone. It was too much to risk.

Eventually I realized that not talking about my loss of faith was creating a wall between us. It still took me a couple of days to gather up my nerve. By the time I spoke with her, my back was knotted with tension.

I told Meg how much I wanted to believe in God, but that my belief no longer rang true. I told her that I couldn't reconcile what had been happening in our family with the idea of a loving God. It was easier to believe there was no God. With tears in my eyes and my voice trembling, I asked, "Would you still love me if I didn't believe in God?"

Her response was swift. "Of course I would still love you. With all the endless searching you have done, if you come to the conclusion that there's not a God, I would believe you. I trust you and will love you no matter what." Then she held me. Filled with gratitude and finally able to relax, I bawled.

Then, knowing that Meg wouldn't stop loving me, I gave up my faith.

No longer did I have to believe that there was a loving God. No longer did I have to reconcile the idea of a loving God with the hell I had been experiencing. I could still hold onto those values that made sense to me. Those that made no sense— that only perplexed and frustrated me—flew out the window. I could be honest and be myself. What a relief.

Then, something strange and mysterious began happening. Over the next few months, I began to sense deep within me that I was loved and cared for. The sense was faint but unmistakable. It wouldn't let go of me. Regardless of what I believed or didn't believe, I knew I was loved. When I gave up my faith, I was given faith.

In my last year of graduate school, I applied for an internship back in Chicago. I was offered a position at La Rabida Children's Hospital on the south side. The first weekend in April, Meg and I flew to Chicago to look for a house. As the weekend drew to a close, we made an offer on the first one we had seen and rushed to the airport to catch our flight. When we called our realtor from the Los Angeles airport, he congratulated us. Our offer had been accepted. That evening, Meg and I celebrated.

Two weeks later, we couldn't believe our eyes. A second test later the same day confirmed it. Faint as it was, the solid blue line told us that Meg was pregnant. Eight and a half months later, our son, Sam, was born on December 22—the first day after the darkest day of the year. Each day afterward became brighter. Twenty-one months later, our daughter, Chloe, arrived and brightened my days even more.

Ask me to explain any of it, and I'll tell you I can't. Ask me if the doubt has stopped, and I'll tell you it hasn't. Then ask me if I have lost the sense that I am loved by something much greater than me. I'll tell you I haven't.

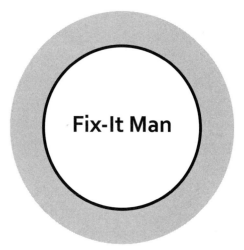

Fix-It Man

A **couple of summers ago, it was really hot, and my** flowers started wilting even though I ran the sprinkler every day. I tried to figure out what was wrong. I eliminated the sprinkler. Water sprayed from all the holes. No stream was inadvertently watering Iowa. Next I scanned the rest of the yard. I stopped when I got to the fifty-year-old maple tree. At the top of the arc, the streams were striking its gorgeous, symmetrically shaped canopy. The water dripped straight down, rather than onto my flowers.

My chest started to swell when I realized I could fix it. I loved being able to fix things. The looks of surprise and gratitude from other people gave me deep satisfaction.

I sauntered into my garage and began assembling my tree trimmer, with its serrated blade and pole extensions. I had the tools. I had the wherewithal. Before long, the water would flow freely, and my flowers would stop wilting.

I began sawing. The problem branch was brushing the ground before I saw the bird's nest. In it were three light blue eggs, one partially hatched. I cursed under my breath. Sitting on a gutter nearby, a mama robin chirped lividly. My daughter, Chloe, would be chirping at me, too, if she found out I had destroyed a family.

Those babies wouldn't last long without their mom, but I knew I could fix it. Carefully, I dislodged the nest and placed it in the sunshine. I cut through the rest of the branch and dragged it out of the way. The mama robin cackled angrily while I raised my step ladder. At the top, I located a branch with a V. It was closer to the trunk, but it would be a solid anchor for the robin's nest. It also wouldn't get in the way of my sprinkler.

I ran into the house and grabbed a headless nail, masking tape, a knife, and some brown twine. Back outside, I attached the twine to the headless nail with masking tape. Then I threaded the makeshift needle and thread through the dried mud and twigs of the nest so that twine hung from both sides. I did the same thing with a second piece. I ascended the ladder and placed the nest in its new resting place. Quickly I attached the nest to the branch with the two strings.

Two minutes later the ladder was in the garage. I had just grabbed a beer from the fridge to celebrate fixing the problem when I heard the mama robin still cackling. She couldn't find her family—the nest was in a different location, now ten feet closer to the tree trunk. How long would those eggs survive without her? I slammed that worry out of my mind, put the beer back in the fridge, and hauled the ladder back out.

I breathed a sigh of relief when I saw the half-hatched baby still moving. I untied the nest and attached it to a branch near its original location. Before I regained my seat on the front steps, the cackling ceased. The mama robin had found her nest.

No lives had been lost. I had successfully fixed the problem once more. I started to think about that beer. Then, out of the corner of my eye, I saw something fall. Leaping from the steps, I discovered the hatched baby on the ground. I looked up. One of the remaining two light blue eggs was hanging precariously from the angled nest.

I started to grind my teeth. Wearing gloves, I returned the hatchling to its nest. Then I propped up the end of the nest with some sticks so the babies would stop falling out. I ignored the mama robin's cackling. I wasn't going to let her down whether she wanted my help or not.

The mama robin flew back to her nest. I waited ten minutes. When I heard no more cackling, I grabbed my beer from the fridge, sat down, and popped it open. I sucked the Bass Ale down with a deep sense of satisfaction. There wasn't a problem I couldn't fix.

Before long, Chloe returned from school. I told her what happened, pointed out the nest, and then told her my day was "for the birds." "Dad!" she chirped. I smiled.

The next morning, I walked out the front door. My flowers looked vibrant, the garden bed evenly watered. I looked at the nest. Mama robin was not there. *She must be gathering breakfast*, I thought. Then I heard her screaming on the gutter again. When she refused to fly to her nest, I climbed the ladder once more. The nest was empty. No eggs. No baby birds. *What's going on?* I searched below. On the ground I found a severed baby bird.

Then I saw the hawk perched atop the electric pole in my neighbor's yard. Had it a pliable tongue, the hawk would have been licking its chops. It was waiting for me to leave. The last morsel of its breakfast was lying in front of me.

I felt as if I had been punched in the stomach. There was nothing I could do. I couldn't fix it. I didn't have the heart to tell Chloe. I trudged back into the house as the mama robin cackled at me from the front yard.

The next spring, Chloe pulled me out of the dirt while I was planting my new flowers. "Dad, come here! Hurry! I want to show you something."

She dragged me to the side of the house. There she pointed to a nest under the eaves resting on top of a bend in the downspout. In it was the mama robin. Chloe and I brought out the ladder to see how many light blue eggs she had laid. We never found out. We couldn't see inside. The mama robin had made sure her brood was going to be safe this time. I smiled for her. Then I smiled for me. I wasn't the only one who could fix things.

Inappropriate Swearing

"S am, time to go!" I called down the stairs.

"Can I come when it's over?"

I could hear "Who lives in a pineapple under the sea?" Sam was watching his favorite TV show, *SpongeBob, SquarePants*. Part of me wanted to go down and watch with him, but I knew there wasn't enough time.

"No, Bud, we need to go now."

I listened, hoping to hear nothing. Instead, I heard the ukulele–slide guitar combo introducing the next sketch. I pulled out my "I mean it" inflection.

"Sam, we have to go NOW."

This time I heard the satisfying sound of silence. A few seconds later, the walls shook as Sam stomped up the stairs.

That's when I heard it. At the top of his voice, Sam swore, "Ass!"

Ass? I thought as a huge, unavoidable grin overtook my face. Why would he use "ass"? A good "shit" would have been appropriate there, but "ass"? I knew I was going to have to teach him how to swear. Otherwise, he was going to embarrass me. He'd never survive the playground.

Now was not the time for teaching, however. Now was the time for enforcing. Sam knew I didn't want to hear him swear. The problem was my grin. I couldn't wipe it off. Sam was so far off the mark in his use of swear words, it was absolutely hilarious. "Ass." His head popped over the half door. I covered my mouth. Sam's jaw dropped when he saw me standing there. He knew he'd been caught.

Hoping he could understand my muffled voice—the grin wasn't leaving—I asked him, "Did you just use a swear word?"

He looked away. In a voice much quieter than the one he had used on the stairs, he replied, "Yes, Dad."

"You know our rule, don't you?"

"Yes, Dad. No swearing."

"That's right, Sam. I don't want to hear you swear."

"Okay, Dad, I won't use any more swear words."

There was a brief silence.

Then Sam continued, "Dad?"

"Yes, Sam?"

"You won't tell Mom, will you?"

"We'll see, honey. Time to go."

Sam left the room to get his jacket. His exit was a blessing, because my grin refused to go away. As the day went on, Sam's inappropriate swearing kept coming back to me. Each time, that huge, unavoidable grin returned. One time Sam asked why I was laughing. I told him I remembered a funny joke I heard at work. He smiled, too.

Then I thought about Sam's request. With another grin, I realized there was no way I could honor it. I couldn't wait to tell his mother.

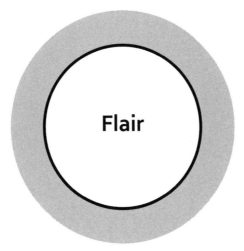

Flair

Back in the '80s, my brother bought a condominium on the third floor at the corner of Damen and Winona in Chicago. Paul was the first owner after the building had been converted from apartments. Unfortunately, while it was a rental, the building had not been maintained. When Paul took possession, it needed work. Especially the kitchen.

The faux-wood cabinets were in fairly decent shape, but everything else required updating. Paul started by patching holes in the drywall. Removing the thirty-five-year-old floral wallpaper above the chair rail and the striped wallpaper below came next. Then a new coat of paint. Next, Paul replaced the chipped Formica countertop and installed a stainless-steel double sink. After he replaced the linoleum floor, the kitchen was fully functional. Happy with the results from his first six upgrades, Paul rested.

Then he got engaged. A basic, fully functional kitchen was fine for a single guy. When a spouse was added, though, basic and fully functional weren't enough. Paul wanted a little flair to spice up the kitchen. Paul and Tina decided to add stylish grayish-white paneling to the lower half of the kitchen walls.

Paul didn't have much time to complete the upgrade. Tina was moving to Chicago in two weeks, and he wanted to surprise her by having it finished. He needed help. My father loved to help his kids with projects, but he was unavailable. Paul knew that I had helped my father panel a couple of rooms in the family home in Minnesota. What Paul didn't know was I had never installed paneling without Dad's supervision. I said I'd be happy to help. I had watched my father enough. I figured we would be fine.

We measured the kitchen and estimated how many four-by-eight sheets of paneling we'd need. I like to have extra material on hand in case I make a mistake. Paul was tight on money, so we bought the minimum. After hauling the paneling all the way up the stairs to his third-floor condo, we caught our breath, ingested more than the recommended dose of pain killers, and began installing grayish-white flair into Paul's kitchen.

We started in the nook because it would require no specialized cuts. We measured and cut the first piece. I quickly squared it to the doorway trim and nailed it to the wall. *Paneling is fun*, I thought to myself.

The next piece required a little more skill. An electrical outlet meant I needed to cut a hole. I'd seen my father cut a thousand holes like that. I followed his steps. Measuring in from the edge and up from the floor, I laid those measurements on the piece of paneling. After the rectangular shaped hole was drawn, I placed the board against the wall to make sure it would be in the right place. There's nothing worse than cutting a hole only to find you've translated the hole into its mirror image—the opposite side of where it's supposed to be. My father always preached, "Measure twice; cut once." To match his actual behavior, the sermon should have been: "Measure six times; cut once—but only after checking one more time just to make sure." I measured again.

I drilled a hole and then jigsawed out the rectangle. I was sure that I had drawn the cutout in the right location. Nevertheless, when Paul placed the board against the wall, I held my breath. I exhaled a sigh of relief when I saw the outlet peeking through the hole. I nailed it to the wall. One hole, two boards so far, no mistakes. *Maybe I'm going to be a good backup for Dad.* As the day progressed, our pile of uncut paneling shrank. We nailed more and more paneling to the wall. Soon we had only one more piece to install. The project was turning out just as I hoped: perfect.

The last piece went between the cabinets and created a backsplash over the counter. It, too, required a cutout for one final electrical outlet. I cut the piece to the right height and then measured for the electrical box. I drilled the hole and jigsawed the rectangle I had drawn, telling Paul, "Almost done." When Paul put the paneling to the wall, the bottom dropped out of my stomach. There was no electrical box peeking through the hole. Paul flipped the piece over and put it to the wall. Now

I could see the electrical box. I had drawn the last hole in its mirror image. I had just committed the cardinal sin my father had preached at me to avoid.

Inside my head, I started to hit myself over and over again for being so stupid. I had not measured six times. I had not checked one more time just to make sure. In my unwarranted confidence and excitement, I had drawn out the piece and cut without question. The result was a huge mistake.

I reminded myself that it was a huge mistake but easily corrected. I just had to cut another piece. I walked into the dining room where the rest of our uncut paneling lay. That's when panic attacked. The pile was gone. Estimating perfectly and under a tight budget, Paul and I had bought the perfect number of boards. Perfect, that is, unless I made a mistake. I made a frantic search in the scrap heap for a piece that would work. To my dismay, all of them were too small.

I started to feel just as small. *Why did I think I could do this project without my dad?* I apologized profusely to Paul, but he didn't seem bothered by my mistake. Calmly, he asked, "What options do we have?"

"We have no choice but to go buy another piece," I said. "I'll pay for it, of course. It was my stupid mistake."

"The Crafty Beaver closed an hour ago," he replied.

"Then we'll go when they open tomorrow."

"Nope," he said. "Tina arrives tomorrow morning. What else can we do?"

Quietly, I mumbled a third option. I mumbled it because it wasn't acceptable to me and I was sure Paul would never go for it. Paul asked me to repeat it.

"We could use the board we have. We could recut the hole in the correct location and patch my mistake with the piece we cut out."

To my surprise and horror, Paul responded, "Let's do it."

I cringed. Paul wanted me to complete the project with imperfection. That was unacceptable. I would always know it was done poorly. It would haunt me. I protested, but Paul kept firm. Finally, I did what he asked.

Carefully I measured six times and then once more before I cut out the piece. With the new hole cut, Paul placed the board to the wall. The outlet peeked through the new hole sitting next to my mistake hole. The white wall behind the mistake was stark. As quickly as I could, I glued in the cutout and caulked the edges to cover the white.

"Looks great!" Paul told me. He was just trying to be nice. I knew the paneling project was flawed. The whole kitchen was ruined. I apologized to Paul over and over again. Eventually, he told me to shut up.

"I think it looks great!" he said. "Tina is going to really like it."

Despite his protestations, I trudged down the stairs to my car deflated and ashamed.

When I saw Tina two days later, she thanked me. She told me how beautiful the new paneling looked. I was sure that, like Paul, she was saying that just to make me feel better. She didn't really mean it. She was going to have to live with my mistake. Though I wanted to apologize, politely I told her that I was glad to help.

After they got married, Paul and Tina kept asking me over for dinner. I always found some excuse to beg out. I kept seeing the cutout in my mind. I knew exactly where it was in the kitchen. It was a continual reminder that I had ruined Paul and Tina's flair. I had no desire to face that misery anytime soon.

Avoidance worked until Christmas, when Paul and Tina hosted the Madvig family festivities. With the entire family attending, I couldn't beg out. At the front door, Paul took my coat. I rushed to the living room, the room farthest from the kitchen. I commented about the comfort of the new couch and wondered if I was ever going to be able to get up. When dinner came, I fought for the seat next to Paul. Paul thought it was because I wanted to sit next to him. Actually, that seat was the farthest from the kitchen. Maybe I could avoid the kitchen all night.

Alas, after dinner, I got guilted into helping with the dishes. I took my time stacking them at the table. Soon I could avoid the kitchen no more. I considered closing my eyes. Dropping the new wedding china might be worse than seeing my mistake, however. Wisely I decided that closing my eyes wasn't an option. Instead, I picked up my pile of dishes, took a deep breath, and walked into the kitchen with one eye closed. As I walked to the sink, I avoided looking at my mistake. I dropped off the dishes and hurried out.

I gathered a second pile of dishes and reentered the kitchen. Again, I kept my eye focused on the sink. As I walked out, however, I found a little courage, and I glanced at the paneling where I knew my mistake was. My brow furrowed as I walked back into the dining room. I didn't see it.

Curiosity overcame me when I went into the kitchen for the third time. Now I had both eyes open. With the determination of one who could always locate all the hidden objects in *Highlights* magazines, I scrutinized the kitchen once more. I still couldn't find my mistake.

Paul denied replacing the paneling. He also denied hiding the mistake behind an appliance. I wasn't sure I believed him, so I kept looking. I knew where the mistake was. I had seen it in my mind all those months. Still, I couldn't find it. Ten minutes later, I gave up. The mistake had blended in. I started to wonder if the glaring error was only in my mind. Maybe Paul was right. Maybe Tina was right, too. Maybe I had done a good job. Even with the imperfection hiding somewhere, the room had flair.

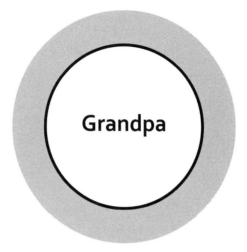

Grandpa

My mother met me at the back door after school. It looked as if she had been waiting for me for a while.

"Grandma Madvig called Daddy this morning. Grandpa fell and hit his head in the garage," she said. "Grandma called the ambulance, which rushed him to the emergency room. Your dad caught the first flight he could to be by Grandpa's bedside. He's up there now."

"So how is Grandpa?" I asked my mother.

"Not good," she answered. "Your grandpa died before Daddy's plane landed."

I burst into tears.

Grandpa's eyes had lit up when I walked in his back door. Grandpa had hugged me to his chest so hard I could barely breathe. Grandpa's strong, thick hands on my back had made me feel deeply loved. Grandpa had loved to play Chinese checkers and hadn't minded when I just wanted to play with the marbles. Grandpa had furrowed his brow when he looked me up and down. He had told my dad he was worried that I was too skinny. He had worried about me! Unlike my other grandparents, he had noticed that I was there.

Barely ten, I had heard about death, but I'd never encountered it. I didn't like it. I knew I would never see the warm smile on Grandpa's face again. I knew I would never be crushed in his arms again. I knew I would never play another game with him. And if I ever added meat to my bones, I would never get to show him. He died worrying that I was too skinny. Now there was a gigantic hole in my heart that he had once filled.

The next day we loaded up the station wagon and started driving. The trip to Minneapolis took forever. My brothers Bruce and John were constantly fighting with each other and then with me over the radio and who got to listen to the headphones. Then I had to dance in line at the gas station while everyone else went to the bathroom before me.

Finally, Mom made the left off Fifty-First Street, and Dad met us in the driveway. I climbed out and stretched my legs. Then I looked at the house. Grandpa had built it himself. I burst into tears again. It wasn't Grandpa's house anymore. Now it was Grandma's house. Dad held me while I cried. It was all so wrong. I wanted someone to bring Grandpa back. *Why did he have to die anyway?*

I gave Grandma a hug when I entered the back door. She gave me a hug, too, but seemed far away. We ate dinner in silence except when my brothers and I fought over who'd get to eat the last of the corn. The next morning, Dad left with

Grandma in Grandpa's—no, Grandma's—car for the funeral home. When the rest of us got there, Dad led us silently into the building. I hated the stale smell. I asked Dad why no one opened the windows. He put his finger to his mouth. When we ran into anyone, they spoke in whispers. I grabbed my father's hand.

Dad led us down a hall and into a room with brown chairs and brown carpeting. On the far wall was a casket. Grandma was looking inside. Dad told us that was where Grandpa was. I burst into tears once more. Dad held me to his side again. Then he asked us to join him as he walked toward the casket. I walked slowly behind my father, wishing I could just get the keys to the car and leave. I wasn't at all sure I wanted to see him.

Grandpa's glasses were the first thing I saw. The dark plastic frames were the same as always. When I got closer, though, I was surprised to find they were the only thing that looked familiar. His skin looked pale. His lips looked too thin. They had on the ugliest color of lipstick I had ever seen. *Lipstick? Makeup? Why is he wearing makeup?*

I said to my dad, "It doesn't look like Grandpa."

"No, it doesn't, does it? It's your grandpa's body, but it's not him."

The tears rolled down my cheeks again. *Why can't it be him? Why can't he smile at me? Why can't he put his hands on my back one more time?* Dad held me until I ran out of tears.

I still miss you, Grandpa.

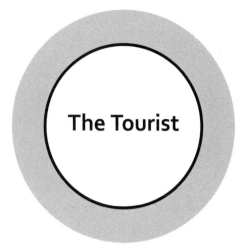

The Tourist

When I climbed into our tiny white British rental car, the steering wheel had been moved. Meg laughed. Red-faced, I walked to the other side of the car, laughing too—a little.

I'd wanted the freedom to set our own schedule. I'd wanted to be a part of the culture, not just observe it. We hadn't signed up for a guided tour; we had stayed on our own in a pub outside London instead. So far I'd taken lukewarm showers on my knees in the tub, gone without meals because we didn't know when stores and restaurants were open, and walked all the way back to the pub from downtown London because we missed the last bus. I'd nearly been killed by a truck because I was looking the wrong way for traffic, discovered that English food was bland and overcooked to my taste, and smacked my head on the ceiling climbing the stairs to our room—twice.

I really hoped that finding the steering wheel on the wrong side of the car didn't foreshadow more trouble on the next leg of our adventure: driving into northern England.

On our way, I wasn't so sure. I only got honked at three times, but we got lost twice. The British road signs may have been in English, but they read like a foreign language.

We finally arrived in York. The lovely room at the bed and breakfast felt like a reprieve. Its window overlooked a lush English garden. Unfortunately my stomach was growling. I couldn't eat English fare again, so we made a beeline for the Chinese restaurant down the street. The thought of rice, soy sauce, and egg rolls made my mouth water. Meg and I sat down in a booth with bench seats covered in deep red vinyl. We ordered our favorite entrée: sweet and sour chicken. It couldn't come soon enough.

When they brought it out, the food looked fabulous. The breaded, fried chicken pieces were covered in carrots, onions, green peppers, and pineapple. I dumped the sweet and sour sauce onto the chicken and popped a piece into my mouth. My taste buds gagged and immediately I spit it out. I dabbed my tongue with my napkin. Then I dabbed it some more. The sauce had no sweet, only sour. It was prepared the English way, tasting of ketchup and vinegar. I swished my mouth with water, and Meg and I ate the white rice and the only two pieces of chicken that had eluded the sauce. We vowed to never order Chinese in England again.

I hung my head as we walked back to the bed and breakfast. Time after time, my dream of being part of the culture was being squashed. The showers were built for shorter people.

British fare wasn't that tasty. Road signs were confusing. But the next day was Sunday, and we were planning to attend a worship service. At least that would be familiar.

After breakfast we entered the old city beneath a stone archway. The crumbled ruins of the ancient Roman wall lay visible on either side. We had no trouble finding our way through the streets to the center of town. York Minster's facade towered above the other buildings. At the west entrance, it took all my strength to open one of the tall oaken doors. Meg and I proceeded down the center aisle, stepping lightly to keep from interrupting the silence. The air was cool and damp, but the candles burning up front by the altar warmed my heart.

It was clear Meg and I were not the first to worship here. The hardwood pew on which we sat had numerous scratches along with "Robert" carved where the bench met the armrest. Some of the scratches looked new; others had obviously been there for a long, long time. Nevertheless, the wood shone. Over the years it had been polished by worshippers' clothing and oiled by the touch of their fingers. The stone pillar next to me drew my eyes upward to the broad, granite arches crisscrossing far above us in the vaulted ceiling. Beautiful carvings of cherubs and seraphs sat where the pillars and arches met. Below were stained-glass windows, each telling a different part of the biblical story. The glory and the majesty were impossible to ignore. I breathed in deeply.

Then the service started. I fumbled through the pages of the Book of Common Prayer but couldn't figure out where the priest had started. I mumbled "watermelon" for the congregational responses—I didn't know what I was supposed to say. After that, I bruised my shin when the woman next to me opened the kneeler. Even in church, I was out of place.

The last straw came when the priest began preparing to serve the bread and wine of the Eucharist. He sang the liturgy not in English, but in Latin. I looked for a way out. Unfortunately, Meg and I were sitting near the front. I wasn't willing to disrupt the worship. Still, I wasn't going to join in when the Eucharist was served.

Soon the people formed a line down the center aisle to approach the priest at the altar. I watched as each of the parishioners passed our pew to go and receive the bread and the wine. Slowly I became intrigued. One man had tears in his eyes. Was he moved by the worship, or had he recently lost someone he loved? Another seemed antsy. Did he wonder if he belonged here, or was he just going to be late for an appointment after the service? A young child standing with her mother appeared unsure. Was this her first time in worship, or did she just want to make sure she didn't make a mistake? One couple couldn't stop smiling at each other. That was love. The woman behind them looked bored. Another seemed annoyed.

I nudged Meg. I couldn't sit in my pew any longer. I had to join the line. Looking at these people, I saw myself. I knew sadness. I knew worry. I knew boredom. They were just like me, even if they didn't do things the way I liked to do them. At the altar, I ate the bread and drank the wine with these people I didn't know. For the first time on our trip, I belonged.

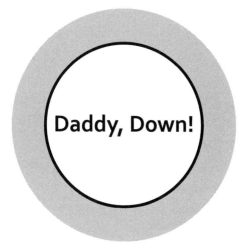

Daddy, Down!

"**A**re you sure we shouldn't bring Sam to the nursery?" Meg asked.

"For the third time, no," I said. "I want Sam to be a part of Chloe's baptism."

Meg and I were sitting in the second row waiting for the worship service to begin. In her white dress, Chloe lay in Meg's arms resting comfortably. Sam squirmed in my lap but wasn't making too much noise. Meg may have questioned bringing a two-year-old to the front of the church, but not me. I was confident that Sam would be fine.

I whispered to Sam, "Hey, Bud. We're about to go up front. I want you to stay in my arms, okay?"

"Okay, Daddy."

I held Sam while we approached the baptismal font at the front and center of the sanctuary. Pastor Bob and my father met us there. Karen and Tim, Chloe's godparents, stood on the other side of the font. I smiled broadly, first at Meg and then at Sam. Chloe was about to be baptized, and all of us were there.

Pastor Bob had just begun the second sentence of the introduction to baptism when Sam said to me, "Daddy, down."

It was a little earlier than I had expected, but I was ready for it. As a clinical psychologist in my growing private practice, I had counseled numerous parents on handling small children in public. I whispered, "No, Bud. Like I told you earlier, you need to stay right here." Then I distracted him. "Look! Chloe's about to be baptized!"

Sam looked at Chloe—for three seconds. Then, again, he said, "Daddy, down."

Five minutes earlier I had been proud of his developing vocabulary. Now I wasn't so sure. "Sam, you need to stay here." I began bouncing him in my arms. I knew stimulation would keep him interested. It did; for about four seconds.

"Daddy, down!" Sam began squirming.

I could have let him down when he began squirming or taken him out of the room. Those are two options I always offer parents. This time, though, he was participating in his sister's baptism. He was involved in a sacred moment in front of the whole congregation. There was no way out. Besides, we had talked earlier. We had an understanding: he was going to be happy staying in my arms; I was going to be happy that I had control of him. Sam's getting down during the baptism would open a whole new bag of trouble. I was determined that he was going to remain where he was.

33 Weeks of Ordinary

I began to hear giggles from the congregation. Part of me laughed inside, too. It really was kind of funny. Then I looked at Meg. She wasn't smiling, and I remembered our earlier conversation about taking Sam to the nursery. I quickly squelched the urge to laugh.

By now, Pastor Bob was asking us to make our vows to raise Chloe as a child of God. Sam continued to squirm. I began to bounce him even more vigorously, holding his legs tighter to restrain his squirming. Then Sam flopped backwards at the waist. Though he was barely two months past the age of two, Sam was a load. That load was a dead weight hanging off my forearm. I had to set him on the ground.

I quickly grabbed his hand. He yelled, "No," and pulled away.

It's going to be okay, I reassured myself. Then I looked at Meg. Scarlet wasn't her best color. I couldn't believe she was getting embarrassed. I began to see red myself: *Doesn't she know this is how two-year-olds behave?* Now I had to worry not only about Sam but also about Meg.

Before he got too far, I grabbed Sam again and raised him back up in my arms. He was going to stay with me whether he liked it or not. Meg had just handed Chloe to my father to be baptized. Five seconds later, Sam flopped at the waist once more. I had to release him, and he began running around the sanctuary.

I couldn't move. I had already used up all the parenting techniques in my toolbox. Thank goodness, Sam saw his older cousin Meghan and ran to her. She grabbed him and quickly sat him on her lap, where she began whispering to him. I started to breathe a little easier. If he wasn't going to stand with us, at least he was sitting with family.

My father put his hand in the water, raised it to Chloe's head, and said: "I baptize you in the name of the Father and of . . ." Sam jumped out of Meghan's lap and ran down the center aisle to the back of the church. Laughter echoed against the walls. Clearly, Sam and the congregation were enjoying themselves. I was not. There was nothing I could do except ride it out, so I tried to enter into the sacred moment. I watched as the baptismal waters flowed over Chloe's head. She began to cry. I just wished it was over.

After my father finished with ". . . the Son, and the Holy Spirit," the organist began playing "Children of the Heavenly Father." Chloe wailed over the organ. My father handed her to Pastor Bob. Bob blessed her. Chloe screamed at him. Then he took her down the center aisle toward Sam, who was still running around. Bob leaned Chloe down. Sam kissed her, and she stopped crying. With a huge smile on his face, Sam ran back up the aisle and into my arms.

As the hymn ended, Pastor Bob gave Chloe back to Meg. Then Pastor Bob and my dad, both smiling broadly, shook our hands. I couldn't get back to my pew soon enough, grateful to leave center stage and let the worship continue without me. Chloe had been baptized. There was no doubting that. Thank goodness, the work of God happens regardless of the behavior of older brothers and fathers who feel helpless to control them.

As I sat in the pew trying to regain my composure, my brother-in-law leaned forward and whispered, "Nice job marketing, Brian."

Waiting for a Call

When I was six, my parents told me that God had called Dad to become a New Testament professor at North Park Theological Seminary. Three months later, we moved to Kimball Avenue in Chicago.

Five years later, Dad was called to teach at Bethel Seminary. Six years after that, he was called to pastor a church in Chicago. Then a church in Massachusetts. Then a church back in Chicago. All my parents had to do was listen. Dad's call was as clear as a bell.

When I was eight, I wanted to be a police officer. I had watched enough of *The Andy Griffith Show* to realize that law enforcement was a worthy calling. Then Uncle Stew asked me how I was going to enjoy getting shot at. I hung up that uniform and began listening for another bell. I bought my red, self-propelled Toro lawnmower with the twenty-two-inch cutting deck when I was eleven. That summer I earned about $50 a week mowing my neighbors' yards in Chicago. Clearly, I was called to be a landscaper.

The landscaping call ended the next summer, when we moved to the Twin Cities. The lawns in Minnesota were three times bigger than the ones in Chicago, but my new neighbors didn't pay any more. I couldn't afford the time or the gasoline to keep my business going. I started listening for a new call.

I entered college as a voice major, but couldn't stand practicing for hours on end alone in a six-by-eight cell. Next up was teaching social studies—and then there were no positions available. Selling copiers followed. When the soles of my dress shoes developed holes from pounding the pavement, I had to make a change.

In 1985, I entered graduate school at North Park Seminary. Seminary scared the crap out of me—especially if I was headed toward pastoral ministry. Would I have to put on a mask and hide parts of me in order to appear pastoral? What did I have to say from the pulpit? What did I actually believe? Would I ever get to see Meg or my future family with all the demands of a church? Despite the questions, I was pretty sure the bell was ringing.

When I told my parents I was entering seminary, Dad's face lit up. He said he'd been wondering when this was going to happen. Mom couldn't stop smiling. Everyone else was supportive, too. It was nice to have the affirmation. I just wished the support would make the questions go away.

I jumped right into my studies. I had vowed never to open a textbook after I graduated from college, but I loved being back in the academic world. I loved exploring ideas. I loved getting to know Brian and Ken and Laura and Rob and my other classmates.

After my first year at North Park, Winnetka Covenant Church hired me as its youth minister. Since I had so many questions, I hoped this part-time job might help me figure out my calling. Each time I preached, I wondered if this would be the Sunday I had nothing to say. Doubts about my faith as well as fears about being swallowed up by all the demands of a church still haunted me.

At the same time, my relationships with the kids in the youth group were very rewarding. I was always spending one-on-one time with one high school student or another. We talked about faith. We talked about the Cubs and the Bears. We talked about the things that bothered them. Our conversations seemed helpful, and I really enjoyed them. It reminded me of what my friend Les told me in high school: I was easy to talk to. Everyone said I'd be a gifted minister, but I wondered if I was being called to psychology. If I was a psychologist, I could help people without having to preach or figure out what I believed.

I applied to five psychology graduate programs. Before long I had interviewed with two. I began the wait to see if I was accepted. At the same time, I made myself "open for call" to serve a church in my denomination. Three weeks later, Meg and I drove to Michigan for a face-to-face interview with a church search committee.

I was direct with the search committee. If they were looking for a pastor who had all the answers, it wasn't going to be me. However, if they wanted a pastor who would search with them, I'd be very open to their call. I had worried that my honesty would eliminate me from their process, but their faces lit up as they listened. The evening was filled with wonderful dialogue and laughter. The next day, the sun shone brightly as we drove back to Chicago. The return trip seemed to take half the time.

When I opened the door into our apartment, the light on our answering machine was blinking. It was a message from Bert at Fuller Seminary. She congratulated me on being accepted into Fuller's doctoral program. I was to begin classes to become a clinical psychologist the following September.

I had just finished listening to Bert's message when the phone rang. It was the church chair. The search committee loved our time together and voted unanimously to have me come and candidate. Unless I preached incredibly poorly at the candidating service, I was being called to be pastor of their church.

I got off the phone and threw my hands up in the air. Calls weren't supposed to happen that way. I had been admitted to a graduate school in psychology. I had been asked to be pastor of a church. Two bells were ringing at the same time, and the sound was deafening. I couldn't hear myself think, so I covered my ears.

The church chair phoned a couple of days later with two potential dates for the candidating weekend. I said I'd talk to Meg and get back to him. An hour later I heard from Bert at Fuller. She was hoping to firm up the list of next year's students. I told her I'd get back to her on Monday. I hung up the phone and began pacing around the apartment. Would I know by then?

I was deep in thought at a seminary gathering that night when one of my professors interrupted my ruminating.

"So how are you doing, Brian?" Fran asked me.

"Terrible!" I replied. I told her my dilemma.

"Well, I'm not sure which way you're being called, Brian, but if you attend graduate school and find that clinical psychology isn't for you, you can quit the program after a year and pursue pastoral ministry. Leaving a church after a year, though—now that would be a whole lot harder. It would cause a lot of pain."

A huge weight fell off my shoulders. I knew which call to listen to. I was going to graduate school. Within a year, I would know if I had made the right decision. I danced my way back to the apartment.

The next day, I called the Michigan church and declined their invitation to candidate. *What a relief.* Two days later, however, seven letters from the seven members of the search committee arrived in my mailbox. Each asked me to reconsider. The letters caught me totally by surprise. I had no idea they felt that strongly. *Did I make the wrong decision? Did I silence the wrong bell?*

I explored my decision with Meg again, spoke with a couple of close friends, and prayed about it. The next day I phoned the chair. I told him how touched and grateful I was for the letters and their affirmation of me. Then I apologized, but again declined the offer to candidate. I felt peace. I had silenced the right bell.

That summer we drove our U-Haul to Pasadena. Though it meant more graduate school, though it meant being more than two thousand miles from home for the next four years, the choice felt right. Two months later, I was sure. There was no question that I loved what I was doing. It was as clear as a bell.

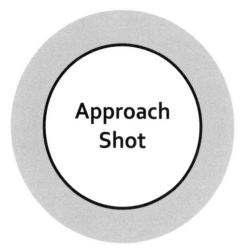

Approach Shot

had to say yes when I got a call from my friend John to play golf on a Sunday morning late in November. Usually by Thanksgiving, snow scrapers and shovels have replaced the putters and drivers in my trunk. Somehow, this year it hadn't happened yet. My reticence to put away the clubs was about to pay off. An hour and a half later, we were teeing off at the Wilmette Golf Club in polo shirts. John drove his ball deep down the middle of the fairway. My drive followed its normal trajectory—low and into the woods on the left. Nevertheless, it was a beautiful day late in November, I was with good company, and I was playing golf.

The trouble started when I began to play well on the back nine. Don't ask me how, but my drives started copying John's: straight and long. After scoring bogey (one over par) on the tenth hole, I parred the eleventh and then shot a three on the difficult par-three twelfth. On thirteen I had a birdie putt (one under par). I missed it but avoided the dreaded three-putt and ended up with my third par in a row. This type of scoring was uncharacteristic for me. I couldn't wipe the smile off my face.

Late in November, the sun set early. I hoped that wasn't a metaphor for how I was playing. As we approached the tee box at fourteen, it was getting harder and harder to see. Complicating matters were my new bifocal contact lenses. While they were going to help me avoid reading glasses, I couldn't see much at a distance. All day my ball went beyond my line of vision. Thankfully, John kept an eye on the ball for me.

The fourteenth hole follows the edge of the golf course. It's short and narrow, and trees hug both sides of the fairway. Usually on this hole I use a hybrid club, the safe shot to keep the ball out of those woods. This time, however, confident with my recent success, I brought out the driver. I was up first. I set the tee in the ground, balanced my ball on it, and completed my warm-up swing. Then I swung. Though I couldn't see it, I knew my drive had returned to its normal trajectory—low and into the woods on the left. John confirmed it. I felt the weight as I could no longer hold up my smile. All too familiar with the set of trees where the ball lay, I knew I was off the par train.

I'm not sure whether John saw my disappointment, but kindly he said to me, "You're gonna like that shot." John reminded me of my friend Joe, who has the ability to see through optimistic eyes. Joe has seen me at my best and my worst while playing golf, yet he always finds a way to see the positive. Optimists can spin good out of any situation—even my golf game.

I didn't believe John, though. I knew the course. I knew I was in trouble. My silent look shouted back, *What? Are you kidding me?* Secretly, I was envious of John's ability to see the bright side. Given that the ball was 200 yards away—okay, 175 yards away—neither of us had any way of knowing what the truth was. Nevertheless, I remained pessimistic. Pessimism makes it easier to avoid the pain of further disappointment.

My shoes suddenly weighed an extra twelve pounds as I trudged up those 175 yards. John repeated: "You're gonna like that shot!" I didn't respond and kept my head down.

I located my ball as we approached the trees. I was correct—my ball rested behind a tree. "You're gonna like that shot!" *Yeah, right!* I began preparing to chip my ball out onto the fairway in order to make bogey. As I readied to swing, however, I looked up to see what appeared to be an opening around the tree in front of me, an opening to the far side of the green, away from the pin. Maybe, with a little luck, I could hit the far side of the green, two putt, and get my par after all.

Sheepishly I mumbled to John, "I might have room." John replied, "I knew you were gonna like that shot!" A smile returned to my face; I hoped he was right. With my nine iron, I took my warm-up swing. I needed to be careful. It would be right up my alley to hit the tree right in front of me. I clearly wanted to avoid that. I took my backswing, came down on the ball, and hit it. I had no idea where my ball flew; my new contacts as well as the darkness prevented me from following it.

Nevertheless, the swing felt pretty good. I just hoped the ball hadn't flown into the woods on the far side of the green.

"I knew you were gonna like that shot!" John congratulated me. Still wary, I asked him: "Did I hit it well?" John smiled: "Three feet from the pin." One hundred and thirty yards out, I couldn't see the ball, but this time I believed the optimist. As we approached the green, my eyes confirmed it: my ball lay three feet from the pin. I didn't get my fourth par, though. I actually birdied the hole.

Afterward, I knew John was right: I did like that shot! I also realized I had a choice: pessimism in order to protect myself from the pain of disappointment or optimism, which makes my shoes lighter. When I'm walking up the fairway, either has an equal chance to be right.

I'm thinking about becoming an optimist.

Good News

Have you ever had a conversation you'd like to have back? Mine occurred when I was a copier salesman at Monroe Systems for Business in 1984.

Unable to find permanent work as a teacher after graduating from college, I had to find a job—Meg and I were getting hitched in three months. I thought sales might be a good arena for my gifts. After all, in high school I convinced Mr. Horn to give up the flattop he'd sported since the '50s. If I could get an Algebra Two teacher to change his hairstyle after twenty-five years, nothing could stop me as a copier salesman.

Over time, I became friends with all the guys working at Monroe. Colin managed us, using fishing metaphors to help us hook unsuspecting sales prospects. We knew where he'd rather be. Ron took time away from munching his unlit (at least in the office) Winston Churchill cigar long enough to teach us how to clear paper jams. Ken, a lifelong Cubs fan, often found himself listening to Rick Sutcliffe pitch the day games rather than making the cold calls needed to generate sales. His sales increased markedly in October after the Cubs' devastating loss to the Padres in the playoffs.

Steve started after I did, so I showed him the ropes where I could. Tall and slender with glasses and a beard, Steve always seemed too smart to be working copier sales. Nevertheless, he started delivering a lot of machines. His ability to be kind and respectful helped in the customer's office. Ultimately, he was just easy to be around. He and I hit it off well.

I began to think Steve might be the perfect person with whom to share the good news of the gospel. After all, if I really believed it was good news, why would I hesitate to share it? I did always hesitate, though. Maybe with Steve it would be easier.

Steve and I had developed a good friendship over the course of a few months. There was common ground between Judaism, Steve's religion, and Christianity—both share the Hebrew Scriptures. Steve would already be aware of the common history, which would provide a solid platform from which to start. Maybe I could find a way to live up to my church's expectation that I share the good news without feeling I was being pushy or arrogant.

One afternoon while Steve and I were delivering a copier to one of his customers, I casually asked, "Hey, Steve. Have you ever read the New Testament of the Bible?"

"I have not," he told me.

My hands started to sweat. This was so awkward. But I'd been taught this was right. I wiped my hands on my pants and kept going.

"Would you ever consider reading the New Testament, the story of Jesus and the beginnings of Christianity?"

"Sure," he said.

"Could I buy you a copy?"

"Yes," he said.

I felt the weight I was carrying lighten. It was working. Here was a polite and respectful man to whom I could backhandedly tell the gospel. I didn't have to say anything directly. I was witnessing to Steve about the good news, and he could decide for himself. Over the weekend, I purchased a Bible containing the New Testament.

When I gave the Bible to Steve on Monday morning, he was gracious and thanked me for the gift. I encouraged him to read it soon because I believed it might really touch him. I showed him the location of the Gospels where he should start, and turned him loose.

Then I waited.

Steve did not leave the Bible on his desk, so I was sure he had taken it home. Each time I saw him, I hoped he would mention he had been reading it. Neither the Bible nor his reading of it came up in conversation. After a month of silence, the heaviness began to return. Had he read it? What had he thought? What if he didn't read it? What should I do then?

One afternoon in the office, in the lull following a particularly funny story, I asked Steve nonchalantly, "So have you had a chance to read it?"

"Read what?" he replied.

"The book I gave you, the Bible."

"Oh. No, I haven't gotten to it."

Someone sharing the good news would never get annoyed, but my throat tightened, and the words came out too high: "Are you going to read it?" My brilliant plan had stopped in its tracks.

"I'm not sure, but I appreciate having the book. Thank you."

To my dismay, Ken heard my voice rise and joined in, "So what if he doesn't read it, Brian?"

I started to squirm. Alarms were blaring in my head. *Look out! Danger!*

"I think it's important he read it," I said.

Ken didn't stop. "What are you saying? Are you one of those people who think if Steve doesn't become a Christian, he's going to hell?"

I hated that question. I hated the answer I was about to give. If this was the right thing to do, why was the knot in my gut telling me otherwise?

I said, "Yes, Ken. If Steve doesn't become a Christian, he's going to hell."

Ken continued, "You're telling me you know Steve is going to hell?"

"Yes," I answered. I held my ground and answered what I had been taught. In my head I believed I was right, but my insides were screaming, "*No!*"

With Ken shaking his head and Steve sitting silently at his desk, the conversation died.

I felt awful. I couldn't get comfortable in my chair. I had been taught to share the gospel, but that conversation was not good news.

In the silence, I wondered what would happen next. I liked Steve. I liked the friendship we shared. How could he remain my friend when he knew I was judging him, his belief system, and his life choices?

Over the next few weeks, my worst fears were realized. Though Steve was always cordial and respectful, he began to distance himself from me. Someone else was already going with him when I asked if he needed any help delivering a machine. He was never hungry when I asked if he wanted to go get a bite to eat. Our friendship vanished. After I quit Monroe to enter seminary, I never saw him again.

I no longer believe Steve is going to hell if he doesn't believe as I do. Hell to me is the absence of relationship, both with God and with other people. "Sharing the good news" with Steve created hell for me. That it bothers me to this day suggests that I continue to be in hell. It is not a comfortable place to be.

The Gift
Beyond All Gifts

It was Christmas morning 1971, and I couldn't wait to open presents. This was a special Christmas, because this Christmas I hoped to get the gift beyond all gifts: an HO train set with a steam locomotive with a smokestack that really smoked, followed by a coal car, two freight cars, and a caboose.

I had always longed for a train set. My older brothers had Erector sets. I was not allowed to play with them, reportedly because I would break them. I wanted a big toy like they had that would move using electric power. I wanted to simply turn a dial to make it go. I was tired of pushing hand-powered trucks and cars around my room.

Page 231 of the 1971 *Sears Wish Book* was the magic page. On it was a picture and description of the HO train set with a steam locomotive with a smokestack that really smoked, followed by a coal car, two freight cars, and a caboose. I found a pen in the kitchen drawer and circled the picture and description. Then I put my name in capital letters next to the circle. Over the next few weeks, I nonchalantly left that catalog open to page 231 all over the house. I left it open on the kitchen counter. I left it open on the nightstand next to my parents' bed. I left it open on top of the bathroom reading basket. After all, this HO train set with a steam locomotive with a smokestack that really smoked, followed by a coal car, two freight cars, and a caboose, was the gift beyond all gifts.

The smartest move I made was getting my dad involved. Dad was the son of a railroad man. His father worked for the Milwaukee Road between Minneapolis and Chicago while Dad was growing up. My dad's soft spot for railroads and trains was my advantage. I casually mentioned to my father, "Dad, wouldn't it be kind of nice to get an HO train set with a steam locomotive with a smokestack that really smoked, followed by a coal car, two freight cars, and a caboose? I might even let you try it some time." In his quiet way, my father smiled and nodded his head.

With everything perfectly planned, you can see why I couldn't wait for Christmas to come. After all, I was about to get the gift beyond all gifts.

When I woke that Christmas morning, my clock read 6:30 AM. Wide awake and ready to go, I hurried downstairs. No one else was up. Waiting was pure agony. As antsy as I was, I found ways to be loud until Dad asked me to pipe down. Eventually, everyone got up to eat breakfast.

When I saw Dad chewing on his last bite of bacon, I announced, "Let's go open presents!"

That's when my mother changed tradition. Out of her mouth came the words: "Wouldn't it be nice to do the dishes first?"

I was thinking, "What, are you crazy?" By the grace of God, however, I was smart enough to avoid saying that. Thinking quickly, I replied, "Sorry, Mom, but that's something new. It's not part of our tradition. Let's follow tradition."

I'm sure she missed the anticipation in my voice when she responded, "Let's do the dishes anyway."

I must admit to getting a little grumpy at this point, but with it being Christmas and all, my mother didn't hold it against me. The dishes were rinsed and in the dishwasher in record time. Soon we were all in the living room under the Christmas tree. Then Mom and Dad started bringing out the presents.

I looked for a package two inches thick, two-and-a-half feet high by three-and-a-half feet wide. Anyone who knows anything about an HO train set with a steam locomotive with a smokestack that really smoked, followed by a coal car, two freight cars, and a caboose, knows that it always comes in that kind of package. When all the presents were out, to my dismay, there wasn't a package two inches thick, two-and-a-half feet high by three-and-a-half feet wide.

I wondered if they didn't get me the gift beyond all gifts. That doubt I put out of my mind as fast as I could. I figured since it was the gift beyond all gifts, it was probably sold out. My parents likely cut the picture out of the *Sears Wish Book* and put it on a card to let me know it was on backorder. As we opened presents, I waited for that card to come. Then the last present was opened. There was no card. Everyone began to leave the room.

I sat on the couch, a frown on my face. I was not going to get the gift beyond all gifts. Was I too young? Was it too expensive? Then, I heard Dad say, "What's this behind the couch?" I looked. He pulled out a package two inches thick, two-and-a-half feet high by three-and-a-half feet wide. Now you may not believe it, but my eyes opened two inches thick, two-and-a-half feet high by three-and-a-half feet wide.

"Why, look," he announced, "it's got Brian's name on it!"

With abandon, I tore off the wrapping. There it was: an HO train set with a steam locomotive with a smokestack that really smoked, followed by a coal car, two freight cars, and a caboose!

My heart racing, I jumped up from my seat to put it together. I left my other presents of underwear and socks under the tree. I figured *that* fun could wait until later. About a half hour later, I finished assembling the oval track and hooked up the transformer. In order to make the smokestack that really smoked smoke, I dripped oil into the smoke hole. Next, I placed the steam locomotive and coal car on the track. The two freight cars followed, and finally, the red caboose. Moving the train back and forth, I made sure all the wheels were aligned. Finally, I was ready to locomote.

I turned the dial on the transformer, giving the train a little juice. I knew from my friend's train that when you did that, only the headlight came on. When the light lit, so did my eyes. I turned the transformer up a little more and heard the hum. I turned the dial a little more, and the steam engine started to chug around the track. After a couple of round trips, the engine heated up enough that the smokestack started smoking. I couldn't believe it. Here I was on Christmas morning, watching the gift beyond all gifts go around the track—my HO train set with a steam locomotive with a smokestack that really smoked, followed by a coal car, two freight cars, and a caboose. Was I in heaven?

I slowed my train to a stop. Then I put it in reverse, and the steam train began to travel backwards. I was careful not to go too fast; there'd be no derailments while I was engineer. I decelerated until my train stopped. After some indecision about what to do next, I started the train forward and watched it go around the track. I watched it circle that oval for five minutes. It circled and circled. My stomach started to feel a little funny. I reversed the train. For a couple minutes, I watched it circle and circle some more backwards. I switched the direction again. Now my stomach was churning. I stopped the engine. Mortified, I came to a realization: an hour after I got it, my HO train set with a steam locomotive with a smokestack that really smoked, followed by a coal car, two freight cars, and a caboose was boring.

After all the planning, after all the excitement, after all the anticipation about getting the gift beyond all gifts, I couldn't believe what was happening. I wasn't prepared for the hole it ripped in my gut. I hated feeling hungry only to discover the perfect meal I had cooked up didn't fill me. My green John Deere tractor and my Mayflower semi-truck had left me hungry in the past, but they were for little kids. This was a big kid's gift. It had all the "mores": more parts, more electricity, more complicated, more expensive. It had to be able to fill me. Yet it didn't. The gift beyond all gifts, my HO train set with a steam locomotive with a smokestack that really smoked, followed by a coal car, two freight cars, and a caboose, left me empty with no hope of having my hunger satiated.

Existentialists have called this emptiness "The Void." Some Christians have called it the "longing for God." Those names were too nice. I called it "The Curse of Christmas Morning." Some Christmases, it haunts me still.

Had I known then that it had a name, that it was The Curse of Christmas Morning, I wouldn't have felt any less empty. The rest of the day was not as I expected. I went back and turned on the train a little later, hoping something had changed. It hadn't. The train still just went around in a circle. I felt depressed, lonely, and disappointed; I couldn't make the emptiness go away. The gift beyond all gifts was just like any other toy. It wasn't going to feed me the way I had hoped.

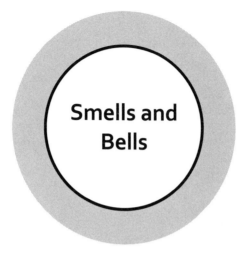

Smells and Bells

hated early morning classes. Eight o'clock was way too early to start the day, especially in early spring, when it was cold and damp outside. As a result, in seminary I was notoriously late to my systematic theology class. I regularly entered the classroom five minutes after Dr. John Weborg began lecturing. Coming in late, I had learned to accept a poor choice of seats in the classroom—"poor" meaning "not near any of my friends."

One day, however, to my surprise and delight I saw a seat right in the middle of my friends. I quickly sat down, trying to be as quiet as possible. Ken gave me a brief smile and then returned to taking notes. Dr. Weborg was lecturing on the "smells and bells" in the worship liturgies of the church. Soon I was taking my own notes.

That's when I heard it. I couldn't believe my ears. The sound was brief but unmistakable: "phrrrft." Flatulence at its fabricated best. Someone brought a whoopee cushion to class and set it off—barely—just enough to make a little "phrrrft." I chuckled. Everyone was too serious in class. I thought they all needed to lighten up. I was always cracking jokes. My friends would just look at me and shake their heads. Now someone else was creating a little fun in class.

I looked at Ken and whispered, "Who brought the whoopee cushion?"

Ken kept his eyes focused on the notes he was taking.

I asked again, "Ken, who brought the whoopee cushion?"

Again, no response. It was obvious Ken was going to be of no help, so I turned to my other side and whispered to Rob, "Who brought the whoopee cushion?"

He, too, didn't respond.

Not knowing who was responsible didn't stop me from giggling quietly, however. I was going to enjoy it. I picked up my pen and fruitlessly tried to take notes on the lecture.

Dr. Weborg continued to speak, oblivious to the commotion in front of him. When he finished telling how incense was introduced into the liturgy, he paused. Out of the silence it exploded: "ppphrrrffffft!" The sound filled the room. Someone had let the whoopee cushion fly.

Dr. Weborg looked up from his notes, a quizzical expression covering his face. I couldn't stop laughing. Someone had the audacity to discharge a Bronx cheer in the middle of John Weborg's class.

I had to find and congratulate the person responsible. The

sound clearly came from behind me. As I turned around to find the guilty party, a number of my classmates stared back at me with confused looks. Not my friends, though. My friends were all jumping out of their chairs. Jumping out of their chairs and rushing away from the second row where I was sitting. Diana opened a window. Rob frantically waved his hand in front of his crinkled nose. Mark looked at me and said, "Madvig, how could you?" Swiftly, I turned around. Dr. Weborg stared at me from the lectern.

There was nothing I could do. Nothing, except sit there and turn a deep shade of red. All of a sudden, a smile overtook my embarrassment. It was April 1. My friends had pulled off the perfect April Fool's Day joke—and I was literally, as well as figuratively, its loud butt.

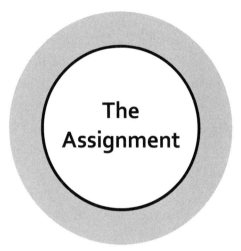

The Assignment

Had anyone been looking in, they would have thought I had threatened Jody's life.

I was wrapping up the first session of a two-day workshop called "Creating Through Loss" at Jody's retirement community in southern Florida. I had just given them an assignment. "Tonight, I want you to create a symbol of your loss. That's your homework for tomorrow."

Jody's eyes opened wide. Her jaw was set. She frowned.

"I can't do it," she yelled from her seat.

"You can't do what?" I asked.

"I can't do homework. I left school a long time ago, and I'm not going back. I hated getting graded."

"Thanks for reminding me. There will be no grades given on the assignment. In fact, I give you all permission to do it badly. You don't even have to do the homework if you don't want to."

Jody slumped in her chair as if she had just been sentenced to a year's hard labor. She wasn't alone. The man sitting across the aisle from her pounded his fist into his palm as he looked me in the eye. The woman next to Jody muttered under her breath about wanting to create something out of me.

I wondered if I had made a mistake in my workshop design. The assignment was supposed to be meaningful and healing. The crowd wasn't getting that. They were getting something, though. They were getting ready to revolt. My heart began racing.

What could I say that would comfort them? "C'mon. It'll be fun." Before they could respond with rocks and rotten tomatoes, I told them I was looking forward to tomorrow morning—I lied—and walked off the stage.

From my corner I watched as the crowd restlessly filed out of the room. I had laid out art supplies to help them create their symbols on a table near the door. Some people picked up glue and old magazines. Others chose modeling clay. Some took nothing. When Jody reached the table, she looked at the art supplies for a moment. Then she looked right at me and scowled as she walked out empty-handed. *Well, that went well,* I thought to myself.

A couple minutes later, Jody returned. Her back turned to me, she grabbed some construction paper and a few crayons, and left again.

I went to lunch scratching my head. Had I asked too much? Had I lost them? Were they actually going to come back the next morning with something in hand? My presentation the next day—in fact, the whole workshop—was based on the homework. If no one did the assignment, I was in trouble. I headed back to my room to create Plan B, just in case.

It had begun to drizzle. I pulled my hood up over my head and counted the cracks in the sidewalk along the way. Then I heard a window slide open.

"Hey!" a voice growled.

I looked up.

From behind a third-floor screen door, the growling continued, "Hey! Just want you to know we're up here working on our symbols. Can't believe you gave us homework!"

A chorus of loud laughter followed. It was infectious; even I started to smile. At least somebody was having fun with my assignment.

When the screen door opened, I couldn't believe my eyes: The growler was Jody. She had a sparkle in her eye and a big smile on her face. She and her friends were in her room working on their symbols together. She waved and closed the screen door. The laughter didn't stop, however. I could hear the fun until the door to my own building closed behind me. Maybe I didn't need Plan B.

The next morning I bit my nails as I waited for everyone to arrive. I dropped my hands into my pockets when clay creations, drawings, and poster-board collages began flowing into the room. Mutiny had been averted. When Jody walked in with her friends, they were still laughing. I smiled again.

After some introductory remarks, I sent everyone off into small groups to share their symbols of grief. Tears and laughter alternated back and forth across the room. When they had finished sharing, I brought them together to wrap up the workshop.

"Thanks for sharing your symbols with each other. It looked like it was a meaningful time for all of you."

There were nods, yesses, and a few "uh huhs" as everyone looked fondly at each other with smiles and red, puffy eyes. In that moment, I had an inspiration.

"Jody?" I asked.

Jody looked back at me, her shoulders straight.

"Would you be willing to come up here and share your homework with the whole group?"

This time there was no fear on her face. Instead, her steely look suggested I was about to be thrown overboard.

"Mine's nothing! Ask someone else."

"Would you share it with us?"

Her friends encouraged her. "Go on," they said and pushed her forward. The room began to clap. Jody looked as if she were dragging an anchor as she made her way to the front. The entire way she fired shots at me with her eyes.

Standing in front of the microphone, Jody opened an eleven-by-seventeen piece of white construction paper. On the left side of the page she had drawn a portrait of a woman: her hair was red, her face bright and smiling.

Pointing at the portrait, she told us, "This is me at fifty."

On the other side of the page was also a drawing of a woman from the shoulders up. This woman had gray hair; her wrinkled face grimaced.

Pointing to this second drawing, Jody declared, "And this is me now at eighty-six. My great grandchildren only know me this way. They will never know this one over here—this fifty-year-old who couldn't wait to shoot baskets with their mom and dad in the backyard as they were growing up, who used to love to play and goof around. I wish I could now, but I can't, even though inside I'm still this fifty-year-old."

Walking back to her seat, she grumbled, "See, I told you it was nothing!"

For me, though, it wasn't "nothing." In fact, it was so much more than "nothing" that I couldn't respond. I was thinking about my son, Sam, wanting to wrestle. I used to love to wrestle with him, but since my back surgery, I couldn't anymore. Inside, though, I was still the guy who could kick his butt on the mat.

Jody sat down, her eyes focused on the carpet in front of her. There wasn't a sound to be heard. In a husky voice, I said to her, "Jody, look around."

She looked. Tears were streaming down cheek after cheek as they returned her gaze.

"Looks to me like you earned an A."

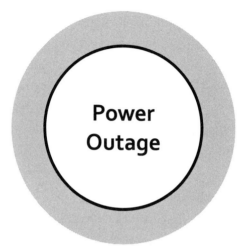

Power Outage

The weather forecasters had been predicting thunderstorms all day. Still, the severity of the storms that blew through Wilmette that afternoon in 2007 took me by surprise. Microburst winds uprooted numerous trees that had shaded the city for over a hundred years. Heavy rainfall filled the deep tunnel faster than I had ever known. With the storm drains closed, the excess runoff created Lake Highcrest where our cul-de-sac had once stood. My umbrella was worthless.

Five minutes after the storm began, our power went out. I told Sam and Chloe not to worry. "Just don't open the refrigerator door, okay?" Power would soon return, and we could resume our regular routine. Usually thunderstorms last fifteen minutes. Blue sky and rainbows replace them soon afterward. These thunderstorms, however, continued nonstop for three hours.

About halfway through the storm, I began to worry about the basement. Only months before, we had replaced the white stick-on tiles with light colored carpet and covered the *Brady Bunch*–inspired paneling with drywall. Surround sound made the whole place rumble. I loved the new theater we had created. Adding a Lake Madvig wouldn't enhance the entertainment experience. I checked the sump pump and breathed a sigh of relief. There was just a trickle of water filling up the pit.

An hour later, however, the water really started to flow. Sam, Chloe, and I began our battle to preserve the basement. Sam scooped water from the sump pit and handed the bucket to me. I passed it to Chloe, who poured it down the cement laundry room sink five feet away. We developed a rhythm. I wondered if I was enjoying it. Before long, I knew I wasn't. The bailing became tedious. There's only so much fun on a water-scooping bucket line.

Meg got home about 9, exhausted and exasperated. Her one-hour commute had tripled because of downed trees and standing water on many of the roads. Soon she, too, was wearing grungy clothes and helping to bail. I kept looking at my watch. Surely it would not be long until the lights came back on and the sump pump started up again. By 10 o'clock, however, I realized we might be in for a long night.

Meg, the kids, and I made a plan: Meg and Sam agreed to bail water for the first hour and a half while Chloe and I slept. At the end of ninety minutes, we would switch. I plopped onto my bed and fell asleep quickly. It seemed only an instant later when Chloe and I were roused from our nap. Meg and Sam climbed into their beds, while Chloe and I, feeling groggy and out of it, went down into the basement. We filled buckets. We emptied buckets. We filled buckets. We emptied buckets. The grind was pure drudgery. By the end of our hour and a half, I couldn't wait to get back to bed and drop my head on my pillow.

Too soon, Chloe and I began our second stint. By now it was 2:30 in the morning. Even with the hour-and-a-half breaks, she and I had been bailing water for over five hours, Sam even longer. The continuous lifting, carrying, and pouring became quite a strain. To my dismay, the radio announced that the power company might not restore electricity for some time. "Some time" couldn't come soon enough. I wanted to be told we'd have power in thirty minutes. Why couldn't we be next on their list? Didn't the power company know we had just refinished our basement? Didn't they know how hard we were working?

During our first shift, Chloe and I had talked about soccer camp. We had talked about how excited our dog is when she meets us at the front door. We had talked about what Chloe's teachers might be like when school started in a couple weeks. This time there was no conversation. My glazed stare never left the floor except to check my watch. I couldn't believe the minute hand wasn't moving. Every bucket I lifted was heavier than the last.

In the midst of it all, I looked up at Chloe. I caught her eye as she handed me the 1,501st bucket of runoff. Out of the darkness, she smiled at me. So full of joy and so unexpected, the smile lit my dark spirit. I couldn't help but smile back.

That smile carried me for the rest of our shift. With renewed energy and determination, I found that the buckets were no longer so heavy. I forgot to look at my watch. At one point our efficiency and speed lowered the water level far enough that we were able to take a two-minute break. During the break, we smiled some more at each other, and she gave me a hug. Drudgery had become fun. Our hour and a half was over in a minute.

When Meg woke me after her next shift, I knew that Chloe's smile was not going to carry us much further. I began searching for an alternative. Meg, Sam, and Chloe kept bailing while I drove an hour and a half north to Racine, Wisconsin. I purchased the last generator Racine had on hand.

Before long, extension cords snaked from the generator on our driveway through the house down to the sump pump. The hum of the sump pump's motor was the catchiest melody I had heard in a long time. The sump pit emptied without the aid of our buckets. Our basement theater had been saved. Meg, Sam, Chloe, and I gave each other a round of smiles and started planning our next movie night. A day and a half later, power was restored.

A night lost its darkness when Chloe smiled in the midst of water-bailing drudgery. It almost makes me want to bail water again.

Almost.

 33 Weeks of Ordinary

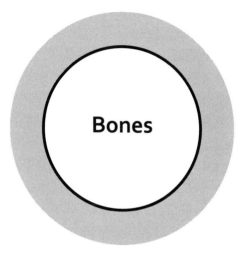

Bones

I **jumped up from my blanket when Les showed up at the** picnic. I hadn't seen him for years and knew I had to say hi. When our eyes met, Les warmly put out his hand to greet me. My whole body shuddered when I grabbed it, though. The last three fingers on his right hand had no skin, only bones. They looked like skeleton fingers.

Les felt my tremor. "I've got a rare and little-known disease. Evidently I was stung by something evil. Then I waited too long to get it diagnosed. Now my doctor's not sure he can help. There appears to be no way to stop it. More and more of my bones are going to show up."

I gave Les a hug. "I'm sorry."

A couple months later, I ran into Les again. More skeleton was visible—only bones were left of his lower jaw; his right hand was worse. I wanted to run.

Then I found myself with two old women in a house. One was trying to put away two skeletons in a closet downstairs. I tried to help, but something kept getting in the way. Then I asked the other woman, "What do you know about Les's prognosis?"

"I'm familiar with Les," she said. "I saw him at the picnic, too. It's tragic. Les doesn't know how bad he has it. There's nothing I can do. He didn't go to the doctor soon enough. Soon he'll be all skeleton."

The idea of Les becoming a skeleton rang in my ears. It rang so loud, I awoke from my dream. I rubbed my eyes clear enough to discover that I was sitting upright in my bed. Relieved that it was only a dream, I plopped back down onto my pillow, but I couldn't find a comfortable position. Les was my best friend in junior high. Though we hadn't spoken for years, we were still close. If something was wrong, I wanted to know. Maybe I could help.

I fumbled in the dark for the light switch next to my bed. When I got the light on, I uncapped the pen sitting there and urgently began writing down the details of the dream for my Jungian class. This was the only dream I'd recorded that had any energy. The first five or six had seemed a bunch of gobbledygook with no connection to reality. I had been wondering if I really bought the idea that dreams could inform our conscious lives.

But this dream was different. My friend Les was in it. The dream suggested that something was going on with him. I approached the professor before class that day to make sure I could present. Regardless of the skepticism I felt about dream interpretation, I needed to find out what this dream was telling me about Les.

When the professor called on me to tell my dream, I stood at the podium and took a couple of deep breaths before I read from my log. Afterward, my classmates asked what associations I had with different parts of the dream.

"Well, Les is a good friend and a free spirit. He took eight years to finish college. During the summer, he runs biking tours in Vermont. Settle down and live a boring life? No way for Les. Les also always challenges my beliefs."

Then they asked me for associations with the disease that was turning his hand into a skeleton.

"Bones remind me of a passage in the Hebrew Scriptures. God promises to put life back into a valley of dry and brittle bones. Skeletons also get associated with death, so I suppose the skeleton means the absence of life." Casually I added, "And my brother Bruce has cancer."

My professor sat up. "Brian, could you repeat what you just said?"

"Sure," I replied. "Bruce has cancer. The doctors are struggling to treat it. They haven't found anything that works yet."

"Do you think there are any connections between Les's disease in the dream and your brother's cancer?" he then asked.

Why is he asking about Bruce?

I had just seen Bruce. Though he had been diagnosed with cancer at the age of thirty-two, the chemotherapy left no visible side effects. In fact, he looked like the Bruce I had always known. The cowlick flipping his thick brown hair onto his forehead still needed regular trims. His gut still protruded far in front of his belt. His smile still showed the caps on his front teeth, the teeth he had lost playing hockey in high school.

Bruce is fine. There's no way this dream is about Bruce.

I started to sweat. I wondered if someone had turned up the thermostat.

"Well, Les's disease has an unknown quality to it, and Bruce has white cell lymphoma. White cell lymphoma is rare. The doctors don't know much about it. The lymphoma is also in Bruce's bone marrow. I guess that could coincide with Les's bones showing," I said.

The room kept getting warmer. I took out my handkerchief to wipe off my forehead. *Why isn't he asking about Les? This dream is about Les!*

My memories with Les were wonderful: Playing Ping-Pong, building bonfires, and drinking case after case of bottled Pepsi while we talked about girls and faith and other deep stuff. I didn't have memories like those with Bruce. He was four years older than me. We'd done some things together, but I didn't feel very close to him. We were growing closer as we got older, but we never talked about deep stuff.

I rolled up the sleeves on my shirt. My voice wavered. "I . . . I don't really think the two are connected."

Softly my professor responded, "I wonder if the connection might be stronger than you think, Brian."

Frantically I scanned the room for an open window. Instead, I saw my classmates all nodding their heads, their faces filled with concern. They had already accompanied me through a number of family deaths. I looked away.

Still, the details of the dream kept racing around my mind. Then I made the final connection: the skeletons the old woman was putting away in the dream. What if they represented the recent family deaths I couldn't put away? The deaths of Grandma Ruth, Uncle Wally, and my brother-in-law Woody continued to haunt me. I gave up fighting. The dream was not about Les. Whether or not I wanted to admit it, the dream was about Bruce.

I sat down. The professor left dream interpretation and began lecturing on the warrior archetype. I wanted nothing to do with warriors bravely standing up to their circumstances. Instead, I wanted to run and hide from my new understanding. I couldn't. My thoughts kept running back to the dream. *What if the dream is right? What if he's turning into a skeleton and I can't stop it? What if Bruce is dying?*

A week later, Bruce was back in the hospital. Six months of chemotherapy had been ineffective, and the doctors were back at square one. They were starting a new round of chemo the next day. I booked a flight to Chicago.

When I got to the hospital, Bruce was watching basketball. Duke was playing undefeated UNLV in the semifinal game of the NCAA tournament. There was no question that we were going to watch the game. Nevertheless, Bruce seemed more subdued than usual.

When Duke called a time-out late in the game, my man-of-few-words brother said to me, "I don't know if I'll ever get out of this hospital. I'm not sure I can beat this cancer."

Bruce didn't look at me when he spoke. Instead, he looked at the toes peeking out from beneath his white blanket. I looked at his toes, too. I had no other response. Giving him a hug or shedding tears wasn't part of the family repertoire. I couldn't say I thought everything was going to be okay. It would have been lying. Though I didn't want to believe it, I had foreknowledge that he might be right.

CBS came back from commercial. Duke's time-out was over, and the game resumed. Bruce's gaze left his toes and returned to the game. I followed his lead. We spoke no more about his situation, though we spent the next two days together. Neither of us knew how. Then I flew back to California to resume my studies. Even if the dream was not predictive, even if he wasn't going to turn into a skeleton, I was very grateful for the little bit of connection we'd had.

Three months later, I got a call one morning from my sister-in-law. Bruce was battling a serious blood infection, and it didn't look good. One by one his organs were shutting down. I thanked her for calling, hung up the phone, and waited. That evening my brother Paul called back. Bruce had died.

I got off the phone and broke down. I cried for his loss. I cried for our lack of connection. I cried because there would be no future together to develop that connection. Yet I was also thankful. Thankful I had been enrolled that semester in a class on dream interpretation. Thankful I had had a dream that told me to take my brother's cancer seriously. Thankful for a wonderful time watching basketball together in a hospital room and an awkward, alive attempt at a conversation neither of us knew how to have. Without my dream about Les, Bruce and I wouldn't have had even that much.

I'm still not sure what I think about dream interpretation. I remain cautious about making connections between my dreams and reality. Nevertheless, I can't deny that once, I had a dream come true.

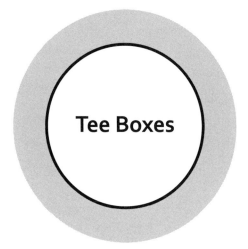

Tee Boxes

After hitting balls at the driving range and putting on the practice green, Steve and I jumped into our cart and drove to the first tee. This was the first time we had played George W. Dunne National, a beautiful but tough championship golf course. I couldn't wait to experience the challenge: water comes into play on ten of the eighteen holes, and the greens, often at the end of a severe dogleg, are huge, fast, and surrounded by sand. Despite my impatience, however, we were going to have to wait. The starter informed us that the tee times were twenty-five minutes behind schedule.

It was only then that I noticed the large sign alongside the cart path. "Recommendations for Tee Boxes," it said. For those with a handicap of three or less, the sign recommended the tee boxes furthest from the hole and the most difficult—the gold ones. The blue tees were for golfers with a handicap between four and thirteen, the whites for a handicap between fourteen and twenty-nine. The red tees, or "women's tees," were recommended for handicaps thirty or higher. My own handicap was somewhere between twenty and twenty-two. That meant I should hit off the whites.

I wondered which tees were hit from the most. Par on an eighteen-hole course is usually seventy-two. Only one out of every ten golfers scores on average below one hundred for eighteen holes. Using a handicap formula, a person with an average score of one hundred will end up with a handicap of twenty-five or twenty-six. Therefore, 90 percent of all golfers have a handicap of twenty-five or more. Only one or two golfers out of ten should be hitting from the gold and blue tee boxes.

Steve and I watched several foursomes hit off the first tee. Slightly cynical about the male ego, I expected a large percentage to hit from the golds, the most difficult tee box. I was wrong. Only one of the sixteen we watched hit from the golds. Then I remembered the unwritten rule: a golfer can't be too arrogant or showy on a golf course with friends. It's not okay to claim you're one of the best if you're nowhere close. Still, fifteen of the sixteen hit from the blues. No one hit from the whites or reds.

Off the first tee, only three of the sixteen ended up long and straight in the middle of the fairway. Eight or ten hit a mulligan, a do-over. A couple ended up fifty yards in front of the tee; a number were in the rough on the left side. One guy was so poor off the tee he lost his ball twice and had to come back and hit a third breakfast ball.

As I waited for our turn at the tee, I couldn't help but wonder: *Why do we men do this? Why do we not follow the recommendations we are given when we play golf? Why do we keep trying to be more than ourselves?* Instead of living with being part of the 90 percent, we try to convince ourselves we are part of the 10 percent who hit from the blues and the golds. We keep dreaming that this will be the round where we finally put it all together. It's not cool to hit from the whites. The whites are the third tier out of four. No one wants to be below average.

There's irony in our decision making, however. Tee box recommendations are set up to improve a player's score. Hitting from the whites rather than the blues or golds should lead to lower scores because there is less yardage to cover. As a result, if a golfer hits from the tees that match his handicap—if he is able to own his actual skill level—he will score better and lower his handicap. For sure he'll have more fun on the course because it feels good to have lower scores. Admitting you are an ordinary golfer and hitting from the whites ultimately leads to less frustration.

Our tee time finally arrived. Steve took a couple of practice swings and then hit his ball long and straight. I put my tee in the ground, placed my ball on it, and swung. I hit from the blues.

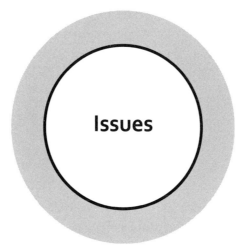

Issues

"**S**o what brings you here, Brian?" Marty asked.

That was a simple question. Maybe therapy was going to be easier than I thought. "Well, the faculty at Fuller Graduate School recommended it. They said it would make me a better therapist. I was also a little curious."

"What would you like to work on?"

"I don't really have any issues," I said confidently. "I'm just here for the experience."

Marty smiled politely. I wondered what that was about.

I met weekly with Marty over the next couple months. One day I reminisced about my singing career: "In high school and college, I sang in choir and performed in small ensembles. Once in a while during a concert, I would take my eyes off the director and scan the audience. My mother always had a serious look on her face. I could never tell if she was enjoying our performance or just yearning for earplugs to eliminate the noise. My dad always complimented me afterward. My mother would nod but say nothing. She was a gifted musician herself. I was pretty sure the silence was critique."

"What makes you think the silence was critique?" Marty asked.

"I always came home with good grades. I never got into trouble like some of my brothers. I was president of my high school choir. I was asked to lead Welcome Week in college. I didn't do any of them well enough, though, to get a 'Good job' or 'I'm proud of you' from my mother. Usually, there was just a comment about what I could have done better." I paused. "I don't know, Marty. Maybe I do have issues."

Marty smiled again. This time, I didn't wonder why.

Six months after I began seeing Marty, Meg's thirty-three-year-old brother, Woody, died. It was the third death in Meg's family in three months. Floored and angry, I flew back to Chicago with Meg to attend the funeral.

Meg's mom and dad asked if I would read scripture. I was only too glad to say yes. On the morning of the funeral, the pastor handed me copies of the scripture I was to read. At the appropriate time, I got up and opened those copies at the lectern. Between tears, I read the passages, hoping to provide some comfort to Meg's family and to myself as we grieved. Afterward, a number of family members thanked me for my reading.

Later that day, Meg and I lunched with my parents at a local restaurant. We sat down to look at the menus, and my mother said to me, "You should read scripture from the Bible, not from a sheet of paper."

I bit my lip and looked down at my menu. During the reading, I had been thinking about making it through without falling apart. I had been thinking about comfort for Meg's family, all of us reeling from losing Woody. Yet, from an aesthetic and symbolic point of view, my mother was right. It would have been more powerful to associate the passages with the Bible from which they had come. Once again, she had found the one thing I hadn't done well.

"I thought therapy was going to be easy," I said to Marty after I told him about the restaurant. Inside, I was being torn apart. *What was wrong with her? Why couldn't she see that I had done well? Was it me?*

"I should have known that I was supposed to read from the actual Bible."

"How were you supposed to know that?" Marty challenged me.

"I don't know, but I should have known. If I'd done it the right way, then she would have told me I did good."

I knew there must be a way to get my mom to praise me.

Another opportunity presented itself before long. This one had promise. Working in tandem with Kathy, one of my fellow students, I had just completed my master's thesis, which looked at marital satisfaction. In our cohort of thirty-five, Kathy and I were the only two to accomplish this feat by the end of our first year. In June, I returned to Chicago with my thesis in my suitcase. I was more than ready to present it to my mother.

The opportunity was perfect. Unlike musical performance, where she could critique me because she was herself a musician, and unlike leading worship, where she could critique me because she had witnessed my father leading worship for years, this was a master's thesis that used complex statistical analyses on psychological factors contributing to marital satisfaction. My mother knew nothing about statistics. She knew nothing about research. I had completed my thesis faster than anyone else in my cohort. She would have to see that my studies were going well. She would have to tell me I'd done well.

In the kitchen of my parents' home, I confidently placed the officially signed and bound copy of my master's thesis on the counter in front of my mother. I stood tall when I told her it was about marital satisfaction. My chest rose when I told her how hard I worked to complete it faster than anyone else.

My mother looked at the thesis with the same serious look she had on her face at my choir concerts. My heart began to pound. Without a pause, she replied, "You really like doing this kind of thing?"

My mind went blank. I didn't know what to think. She'd done it again. She had found a way to critique me. Then, inside, I started to laugh. It wasn't the laughter of insanity or delirium. No, it was the laughter of insight. At that moment I realized it was never going to happen. I was never going to get the approval I hoped for. My mother was just not put together that way. Expecting her to do something she was not capable of was folly. And if it was something she was not capable of, I could finally stop trying to get her approval. A deep sense of relief flooded over me.

I couldn't wait to get back to California. At my next appointment, I told Marty about my mother and the thesis. This time, we smiled together.

And then I burst into tears.

"Marty, I still wish she could affirm me just as I am, without critique. I still wish she could tell me I am talented and gifted. I still wish she could love me the way I want to be loved."

"You've given up a lot," Marty responded.

"Yeah," I said. "It feels like I've lost my mother—or at least, the mother I wanted." I paused for a moment and dried my cheeks. Then I looked at Marty. My smile returned. "I can't believe I told you I didn't have any issues."

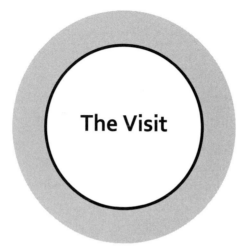

The Visit

I couldn't stop thinking about my mother as I drove to the Twin Cities. I had gotten on the road forty-five minutes later than I had wanted. Now I was stuck behind a truck. The commuters rushing to work ignored my turn signal, keeping me out of the fast lane. It had just started, but my trip was already taking too long.

My sister, Karen, had tried to assure me my mother's stroke was minor. I wasn't so sure. The stroke signaled the beginning of the end of my mother's life. Any day she could have another. At any moment she could die. When the traffic finally cleared, I accelerated .

As noon approached, I was driving past the Wisconsin Dells. Usually I reminisce about riding the amphibious World War II–era Ducks, wiping the burn from my eyes at the chlorine-thick water parks, or being dazzled by Rick Wilcox magic. Not this time. All I could think about was how frustrating it was to be only halfway there. I was living up to my family nickname, "Leadfoot." I pushed my right foot further toward the floor.

As I drove, I called all my siblings. When my brother Bruce had died, most of my family seemed caught unaware. His death just crept up on us. I didn't want that to happen again with Mom. I wanted everyone to be aware it was coming. I wanted everyone to have a chance to speak with Mom before it was too late. That included me. I started to think about what I wanted to say. I took a couple of deep breaths. My blood was speeding almost as fast as my car.

By the time I finished the calls, I had passed Eau Claire, Wisconsin, my three-quarters marker, and was crossing the St. Croix River into Minnesota. A half hour later, I slowed as I walked down the hospital hallway to my mother's room. Now I would see for myself how she was. Mom smiled at me, and I hugged her. Though she struggled to find words, Mom seemed fine. Maybe my sister was right.

I spent the next couple of days answering Mom's questions about my family and my work. The knots in my muscles loosened, and I breathed a little easier. Her doctor showed me the damage on the CAT scan, confirming that the stroke was minor. Speech therapy was helping her find new ways to communicate. Mom's chances of having a second stroke had greatly increased, however. She could have another at any time.

Saturday was my last day with Mom before I had to drive back to Chicago. The evening approached; soon it was time to go. I embraced Mom and said, "See you later." Dad walked over, gave Mom a kiss, and said good night. Together he and I walked out of the room.

It wasn't until I passed the nurses' station that I realized what had just happened. I had conveniently forgotten what I had told my siblings as I drove past the Dells. I hadn't told Mom what I had thought about in the car. What if this was my last chance? I told my dad to hang on.

I walked back into my mother's room.

"Did you forget something?" she asked.

"Yes," I said, and sat down on the side of her bed.

I leaned uncomfortably on my right hand, looked her in the eye, and opened my mouth: "Mom, this may be the last time we see each other."

Mom met my gaze, but her eyes opened wide. It was clear that she was uneasy with the direction I was taking this conversation. She tried to interrupt.

"No, Mom, one of these times when I leave, we won't see each other again. It may not be this time, but it is going to happen." Tears streamed down my cheeks. "Thank you for being my mother, for raising me well, for giving me a good life. I will always be grateful for you and grateful for what you have given me. I love you, Mom."

I knew in my heart that Mom cared, but she shed no tears. She smiled and said, "I love you, too, Brian." We embraced one more time, and I left. Wiping the tears from my eyes, I gathered up my father and walked out to the car. The next day I was back in Chicago.

Two years later, Mom has had no further strokes. At the end of a visit, I leave in my usual, matter-of-fact way: "We'll see you, Mom and Dad. Thanks for opening your home to us. I love you." Each time could be the last time. I wonder if I should say more, but I don't. Nevertheless, in my mind is the memory of an intimate, awkward moment when I told Mom I loved her and she told me she loved me. It was our first good-bye.

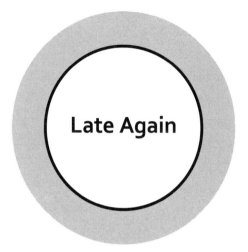

Late Again

Late again! I tossed aside the book I'd gotten lost in and leapt off the couch.

"Sam," I yelled. "Hurry up! Get ready. You've got practice."

"Okay, Dad."

In five minutes, eight-year-old Sam was supposed to be standing at first base on a baseball field ten minutes away. For every five minutes he was late, his coach reduced the number of innings Sam played in the next game. On top of that, I was scheduled for an important bagel-and-cream-cheese meeting with a business associate immediately after dropping Sam off.

I tried to minimize the damage. I rushed to Sam's room to help him get ready. Unfortunately, genetics don't fall far from the tree. Sam was dawdling. I yelled at him to hurry up. I had to prompt him twice to don his grass-stained white knickers. Then he couldn't find one of his socks. After the missing sock was discovered in his sister's room, he had to turn both right side out. Finally, Sam slid his socks over his toes and onto his feet.

Sam was oblivious to the time it was taking him to get ready. I wasn't, and my temperature started to rise. I knew his playing time in tomorrow's game was dwindling. I knew my business associate was soon going to wonder where I was as his coffee got cold. I found my right arm windmilling, hoping it might help Sam speed up. Eventually, he was dressed and carrying his mitt and baseball bat. On the way to the car, I rubbed his head. "Stop," I said. After a frantic search through a pile of dirty clothes back in his room, we found a baseball cap to cover his buzz cut.

Backing the car out of the driveway, I headed down Highcrest Drive dangerously close to the speed limit. All right, I was speeding. I made the first left onto Illinois Avenue. After the second left, I settled into the routine of driving to Sam's practice, and my mind began to wander. It wandered right to the file I needed for my bagel-and-cream-cheese meeting. Unfortunately, my wandering mind could see the file sitting on the kitchen counter at home. I looked at the passenger seat next to me. I wanted evidence that it was only a daydream. The seat was empty.

"Shit!" I yelled out. As I slowed to make a U-turn, I looked in my rearview mirror to make sure there were no cars behind me. There was Sam sitting in the backseat playing a video game. I had forgotten about him. I swore again, inside. Not only was I making him late, now I was cursing in front of him.

I didn't have time to think about my poor parenting as I sped back to Highcrest Drive. Before long the folder was sitting on the seat next to me, and we were headed back toward the baseball field. After catching my breath, I decided it was time to reclaim some of my parenting ability. I looked at Sam in the rearview mirror as we waited at a stoplight.

"Hey, Sam!" I said.

He looked up from his video game and said, "Yes, Dad?"

"Sam, I'm sorry. I didn't mean to swear in front of you. That's not something I should have done."

"That's okay, Dad," he said as his eyes returned to his game. "You do that all the time."

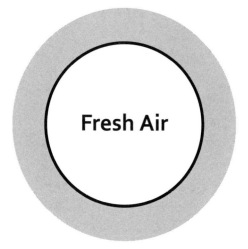

Fresh Air

Playoff fever was in the air. It was a cold Minnesota Friday night when our Mounds View Mustangs were scheduled to tip off against the Anoka Tornadoes for the conference championship.

It was my turn to drive, so I picked up Minnow, Merc, and the Beav and drove the forty-five minutes to Anoka. The game was awesome. Down at the half, Van, Rich, and Luke rallied the team in the fourth quarter. They won by two points. Our next stop was the state high school basketball tournament.

We left the gym high-fiving each other and climbed in the car. The needle on the Gran Torino's gas gauge was flirting with empty. I pulled into a gas station and pumped ten gallons in the tank. Behind the counter was a display filled with cheap cigars. Suddenly, two voices started bickering in my head:

"Wow! Cigars on the ride home."

"What are you, crazy? You know you can't smoke in the car!"

"Why not? What a great way to celebrate! We won the game!"

"Why not? Because Mom will kill you!"

"Oh, she'll never know. We'll just roll down the windows."

I strutted back to the Gran Torino and flashed the five-pack of Swisher Sweets in front of my friends' noses. The Swisher Sweet was our cancer stick of choice. The rum-flavored end more than made up for the harsh taste. Besides, a five-pack cost only a buck seventy-nine. Minnow, Merc, and I happily removed the cellophane wrappers. The Beav handed his back—he was in one of his nonsmoking phases.

I pressed the lighter into the dash. The red hot end glowed in the dark. We lit our cigars. Despite the open windows, smoke filled the car. The Beav pursed his lips, rolled his eyes, and stuck his head outside. While he was turning green, Minnow, Merc, and I laughed. Then we asked if he wanted to change his mind and join us, but he refused. We didn't care. It was his loss. We were in high school, and we were smoking cigars. The car was cold in spite of the heater blasting, but the ride home seemed like it was over in a minute. Despite all the coughing and spitting out the windows, and the Beav turning green, it was a grand experience in my Gran Torino.

By mid-morning the next day, munching on my second bowl of Cap'n Crunch, I had already forgotten about the cigars. Then the front door opened. My mother marched right over to me.

"Brian, was someone smoking in the car?"

Evidently keeping the windows rolled down had failed to air out the evidence. Seeing no way out, I told the truth. "We smoked cigars to celebrate after the game."

Fifteen seconds passed. My mother was surprisingly calm. She said, "You know I have asthma. Even the smell of smoke makes it hard for me to breathe."

She walked to the closet to put away her coat. I felt like the worst son ever. I had forgotten about her asthma. My mind also raced over the punishments she was surely considering. I was pretty sure a spanking was out. Putting a six-foot-five-inch sixteen-year-old over her knee seemed unlikely. I wasn't sure, though. She was resourceful. A second and more likely punishment was the evil eye. My mother could give a look that made me feel three feet tall. Getting the evil eye was worse than being spanked. When she walked back into the kitchen, I wished I could hide.

Then she said to me, "Don't smoke in the car again. Go and get the Lysol out of the bathroom. I want you to spray the inside of the car."

Then she left me to my Cap'n Crunch.

I couldn't believe it. No spanking? No evil eye? I only had to spray air freshener inside the car? I gobbled up my now soggy cereal and carried my dishes to the counter. I even rinsed and put them in the dishwasher. I had no desire to give her a reason to change her mind. Then I grabbed the Lysol, the car keys, and my coat and headed outside.

Soon all four of the Gran Torino's doors were winged open. I hoped the fresh cold air would help eliminate the smell of smoke. As I began spraying, my nose crinkled. The scent was worse than the cigar smoke. I knew it would make my mother happy, though.

While I was spraying, I heard footsteps on the driveway. Dad had walked home from work. Mom was preparing soup and a sandwich for him inside. As he approached, my throat began to feel dry. My father was always responsible. He knew he had to be a role model to his children. He took discipline seriously.

He stopped next to me. Cordially he said, "Hi."

"Hi," I responded, warily.

"What are you doing?"

I offered a minimalist response: "Spraying Lysol in the car."

I hoped it would be enough. It wasn't.

"Why are you spraying Lysol in the car?"

I mumbled under my breath so he couldn't hear it, "We smoked cigars in the car last night."

"What did you say?"

Gathering a deep breath, I told him: "Minnow, Merc, the Beav, and I smoked cigars in the car last night. We celebrated after the basketball game. Can you believe we're going to the state tournament?"

My father stood silently waiting for me to continue.

"Mom asked me to spray Lysol because the car smelled and bugged her asthma."

Then I waited, sure my sentence was about to be pronounced.

"You know you shouldn't smoke in the car," my father said to me.

I nodded.

"You know it makes it hard for your mother to breathe."

I nodded again.

"Then make sure you spray the car really well."

I stood there dumbfounded. Was that all? Wasn't he angry? Where was my sentence?

As my father turned his head toward lunch, I thought I saw a smirk on his face. It didn't make sense—a smirk was so out of character. I looked a second time. By then, my father and his smirk were gone. I stood there dumbfounded once more. Had my father really smirked? Was it possible he remembered what it was like to be a teenager? Was there still a little imp inside him?

My chattering teeth soon brought me out of my stupor. I finished spraying the Gran Torino, closed its doors, uncrinkled my nose, and walked into the house to join my mother and father. My heart was already warm, but I wanted some soup to thaw the rest of my body.

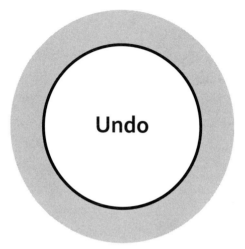

Undo

"Hi, Dad! This is Chloe. I got two 'excellents' on my book report. I know you're really proud of me—that I got two 'excellents' on my book report. And Miss Dietrich gave me some really nice comments. Bye. I love you. I LOVE YOU!!"

For six years, that voice message was on my machine at work. When Chloe first left it, I smiled. Whenever I listened to it, I smiled. If I needed a pick-me-up, that message provided it. The message carried me through a lot of years and a lot of times. The joy in Chloe's voice was a gift. It connected me to a fondly remembered time. It connected me to a little girl who couldn't wait to let her dad know how she did in school. It was a continual reminder that I was loved.

One day while trying to rush through my voice-mail messages in the midst of a chaotic schedule, I accidentally erased the message. As soon as I pressed the button, I knew that I had erased Chloe's voice. I tried to get it back, but couldn't. There was no way to undo it.

That it was gone didn't surprise me. I knew it would happen sometime. I had already imagined a voice-mail system crash leading to its loss. I had already considered I might accidentally erase it myself. I didn't know that there was a rugby team ready to smash me in the gut as soon as I pressed the button. I didn't know how hard it would be to hold back my tears. I wanted to get mad, to fight and thus undo what happened, but it would have been fruitless. My stomach ached.

I wanted to make the ache go away. I looked in the system manual, desperate to find that I was wrong. Maybe the message wasn't really gone. Maybe I had missed something about undoing accidentally deleted messages. Unfortunately, there was nothing.

Since the manual was no help, I tried to make the ache lessen by thinking it away. I thought about the class I taught encouraging people to create through their losses. Maybe I could create out of this loss. My thoughts didn't help, though. I didn't want to create. The ache remained.

Somehow I had to erase the pain. Maybe Chloe could give me relief. She'd already been a pick-me-up with the message. When I woke her the next morning, I told her I erased the message. I hoped I might get a "That's okay, Dad" from her. I didn't. Instead, she said nothing and looked away. I left her as she got ready for school. My gut continued to ache. When she walked into the kitchen a few minutes later, I could no longer hold back the tears. I thanked Chloe for her message, for sending it to me, and for liking me in the first place enough that she wanted to send it to me. My stomach seemed to settle a bit.

The next morning on the way to work, I called for messages. A minute ray of hope flickered that I would hear, "Hi, Dad. This is Chloe," again. I tried to be patient as I listened to all the new messages. Finally, the last new message ended. I played the first old message, hoping to hear that familiar, joyful second grader's voice. Instead I heard the voice of Dr. McCann referring a new client to the practice. Chloe's message was gone.

Eventually it won't hurt so much, I hoped. *Eventually, I will find a way to create out of this.* Right then, though, I just wanted it back.

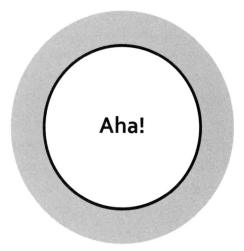

Aha!

"**D**ad, where do Uncle Bob and Aunt Barbara go to church?" I asked from the backseat.

"They don't, honey. Your mom and I keep praying, though. We hope it will change."

"Why, Dad?"

"Because if they don't accept Jesus, they won't get into heaven."

I knew what that meant. It meant that my Uncle Bob and Aunt Barbara were going to H-E-double-toothpicks. My heart sank for my aunt and uncle. I really hoped Mom and Dad's prayers would get answered.

A few years later, I was big enough to ride in the front seat. I couldn't touch the AM dial, though. My father knew rock 'n' roll wasn't music. I didn't question him until the deejays started playing Elton John's "Rocket Man" on the radio. That song was cool. I tried to get him to listen to the song. I hoped it might change his mind about rock 'n' roll, but he refused. He couldn't understand why anyone would listen to that tommy-rot. I was glad when my older brother rigged up headphones in the car. Then I could listen to "Rocket Man" even when my dad refused to.

When I was in high school, on Tuesday mornings at 6:30 AM, Les, the Beav, Merc, Tanya, Dobee, and I would gather for breakfast and Bible study with Mal and Don, our Young Life leaders. We'd get into great debates about what the Bible said and what the Bible didn't say.

Les questioned me one day, "Moose, what about the people who have never heard the biblical stories? The ones that live in remote places?"

"Les, the Bible says that Jesus is the only way to God."

"I don't believe that's right, Moose."

I wanted to believe like Les. I hated that there were people like me and my family who were "in" and people like my aunt and uncle who were "out." I hated telling others that I knew the one and only right way to believe. It seemed incredibly arrogant to believe those things. I couldn't believe like Les, though. My father believed Jesus was the only way to God. It wasn't like "Rocket Man." No headphones could drown out my father's voice. He knew his stuff and had the qualifications to prove it.

My father was a biblical scholar. He helped translate a new version of the Bible into English. Over and over I heard his seminary students tell me how influential he had been in their spiritual development. Even though it made my stomach churn, I couldn't doubt my dad. Doubting my dad meant I would join my aunt and uncle in H-E-double-toothpicks.

During my first year of doctoral studies in psychology at Fuller Seminary, I was daydreaming in class one day. The guest lecturer had just finished explaining three different ways to treat depression when the "Aha!" moment slapped me awake.

I'm not going to hell! Even if I don't believe what my father believes, I'm not going to hell!

There were three different ways to treat depression. There were different ways to interpret the Bible. I couldn't believe it. It seemed so simple. In fact, many highly respected scholars who read the same biblical texts as my father had come to different conclusions. Who was to say who was right? If there wasn't one, and only one, answer, then I was free to ask my questions. And free to come to different conclusions.

As soon as class ended, I accosted my friend Tim. Tim knew all about my struggles, so I had to tell him what happened. He was excited for me. My insight made sense to him. Then I told Meg. And I remembered I was traveling to Chicago in two weeks. I could also tell my father. Finally, I had a way to handle our differences. I could tell him we were in different places theologically, but the differences didn't need to create more distance between us.

When I got to Chicago, I asked my father out to the Golden Nugget for breakfast on Saturday morning. Sitting at the table waiting for our coffee to come, I realized the tips of my fingers were hurting. I had nibbled my nails to the quick on the drive over. I reminded myself that I was looking forward to this conversation.

After some small talk about the trees starting to bud and the hope that spring was just around the corner, I took a deep breath.

"Dad, I've been doing a lot of thinking. I've been thinking about Jesus being the only way to God."

My father listened quietly.

I continued, "Dad, I think Jesus might be the best way, but I don't believe he's the only way anymore."

Without hesitation, my father responded: "Then you're telling me that I'm wrong."

"No, Dad," I countered. "What I am telling you is I can no longer believe that Jesus is the only way, but that doesn't mean you have to believe what I believe. We can believe differently."

"Then you're telling me that I'm wrong."

Hoping it might help us see eye to eye, I told him about my "Aha" moment. That didn't work, so I tried to convince him intellectually. Next, I tried using metaphor. Try as I might, nothing got through. His ears were closed. Finally, I gave up. We were both silent for the rest of the meal. I never finished the pancakes sitting in front of me.

I walked out of the restaurant not sure where I was going. I couldn't believe it. I couldn't believe my father couldn't hear what I was trying to tell him. I couldn't believe that the answer I came up with, the answer that was going to lessen the distance between us, actually created more. And I couldn't believe how scared I was. What if I was wrong?

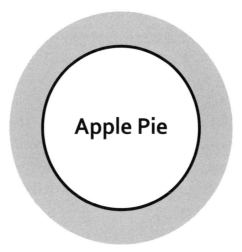

Apple Pie

Dad, are you seeing what I'm seeing? I didn't let the words out of my mouth. Mom sat propped up in her hospital bed. Dad and I had been talking with her for three hours. She had some trouble finding words, but my mother's mood was upbeat.

Are you seeing it, Dad? Mom had just had a stroke, yet she seemed happy-go-lucky. The gravity of the situation didn't seem to affect her at all. It was almost as if Mom were younger, almost as if she had become a child. I was glad she wasn't as worried as I was. Still, I wondered if the stroke was more serious than we had been told. Had the stroke destroyed the part of her brain where adulthood resides?

Dad and I didn't talk about sensitive, vulnerable subjects. Eighteen years had gone by since the last time we talked about something that really mattered. My stomach always churned when I thought about the broken connection, but I had learned to accept that Dad and I just didn't go there. Now my stomach was doing somersaults.

When the orderly delivered Mom's dinner that evening, Dad and I went downstairs to get our own. We filled our trays in the cafeteria line and found a table next to a window looking out on a patio garden. We sat in silence for ten minutes while we picked at our plates. My stomach continued its gymnastics. Finally, I couldn't keep quiet any longer. It was lonely worrying about Mom by myself.

"How are you doing, Dad?"

"Okay."

I sat waiting. I hoped he would fill out his answer. I really didn't want to pry. A couple minutes later, I realized "okay" was all he was going to say—prying would be required if we were going to have a conversation. I hesitated. *Do I really want to do this? Do I want to chance reopening a deep wound? Do I want a potentially even wider chasm? Or do I try to bridge the gap between us?*

"Dad, I noticed that Mom seems younger."

Tears welled up in his eyes. Then he looked at me, and our eyes met for the first time in years. "Yeah," he responded. "I noticed that too. I don't know what to do. I'm really worried she'll have another stroke and die. I hate to confess this, but there's a selfish part of me that has always wished I would be the first one to go. I don't know how I could go on without her."

My own tears began to pour out. The tears were for my dad and what he was experiencing. The tears were for my mom, who just had a stroke that might be more serious than we knew. Mostly, though, the tears were for what was happening between me and Dad. It was the first time we had ever cried together. I felt closer to my father than I had since the time I was small enough to climb into his lap.

We sat in that cafeteria trying to avoid drawing attention to ourselves. I'm not sure it worked. I had to snag extra napkins off the table next to us. They got drenched before long, so I had to grab some more. Eventually, the tears stopped. I looked over to Dad, and he smiled at me. I smiled back.

Then he said, "We'd better eat this pie and get back to your mom."

I willingly obliged. My appetite had returned. Ten minutes later, we were at my mother's bedside.

"Where have you been?" Mom asked.

"We had dinner in the cafeteria," my father answered. "The apple pie was good."

I nodded. Mom changed the conversation to her favorite football team, the Green Bay Packers. I rolled my eyes and laughed. The evening seemed over in a minute.

During the ride home that night, my father said to me, "You know, our time in the cafeteria felt really good. I usually don't share how I am feeling with anybody. I kind of do it by myself, but it was really nice to be able to share it with you. Thank you."

"Thank you, Dad," I said. "It meant a lot to me, too."

A minute passed by. Then I asked him, "Hey, Dad. Is that really true? Do you always do it by yourself?"

He responded, "Yeah, that's probably true."

"Dad," I said, "it's probably time to stop the do-it-yourself projects."

I think I saw him nod. We rode the rest of the way home in silence.

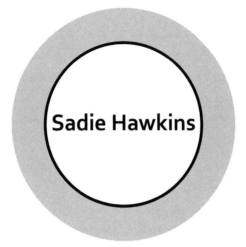

Sadie Hawkins

TP-ing their house the afternoon of the dance was my idea. Steve and I purchased six four-packs of Charmin at Penny's Supermarket on the way to Tanya and Teresa's house. We quietly laughed as we threw roll after roll into the trees. I couldn't wait to find out what Tanya's reaction would be when she got home from school—when she discovered the trees on her hillside covered in soft, white, two-ply beauty. It would be a unique experience. No one ever got TP-ed in the middle of the day.

Twenty-one of the twenty-four rolls were already draped in the trees when I heard the shotgun cock. I looked up the hill. On the driveway above us stood a man. His jaw was set. His mouth looked stern. His eyes were focused on us. While the barrel of the shotgun in his hands was raised toward the sky, it wouldn't take long to point it at us.

"Run! He's got a gun!" I screamed at Steve. I loped down the hill. Luckily my car was on the road just below us. Steve was still closing his door when I floored it. I didn't stop until we were on the far side of Shoreview. I waited for my heart to slow down.

I looked at Steve. "Was that their dad?"

"I don't know. I've never met him."

"Me neither," I said. "I hope we didn't just screw it up."

Tanya was one of my nicest friends in high school. She was also one of the prettiest. Her eyes sparkled when she looked at you. Her smile lit up the room. Her long red hair flowed from side to side as she walked down the hallway. I had a perpetual crush on her but never had the nerve to ask her out. She was out of my league.

Both my sophomore and junior year I hoped she might ask me to Sadie Hawkins. Both years she asked someone else. Each time on the gym floor she smiled at me as she square danced with her date. I couldn't stop wishing I was the one doing the allemande left with her. By the time my senior year came around, however, I had already given up hope. It wasn't going to happen.

Then she walked up to me before class. Her smile lit up the hallway. I was sure she was going to ask me about the World History homework.

"Brian, are you doing anything a week from Friday?"

I felt my heart jump. "I don't think so."

"I was hoping you could go to Sadie Hawkins with me."

"I'd love to!" I responded immediately.

I couldn't stop smiling the rest of the day. Or the next week and a half, for that matter.

Now, hours before the dance was to start, Steve and I had sent her father into a rage. He had just threatened to pepper our butts with birdshot. The afternoon wouldn't end. I couldn't stop cursing under my breath. I was sure Tanya was going to call and tell me her father refused to let her go.

The call hadn't come by the time I picked up Steve. In silent dread, we drove over to Tanya and Teresa's house. I didn't want to meet her father. I parked my beige Gran Torino at the bottom of the hill. I hoped our getaway car wouldn't be recognized in the dark. I wasn't sure if I should enjoy our artistry as we passed by, but the soft, white two-ply looked quite lovely.

At the door, I drew in a deep breath and fumbled for the doorbell. Tanya opened the door and asked us in. She looked beautiful in her straw hat, freckles, pigtails, and denim overalls. I wanted to get the girls and go, but she announced that her parents wanted to meet us. My heart sank. I looked around for the shotgun.

Tanya led us into the living room. Her father sat behind a newspaper on the couch. Her mother rose to meet me. She was gracious and nice. I breathed a little easier. Then Tanya dragged me over to her father.

"Dad, this is Brian."

He looked at me over his newspaper. Then he quietly folded it and laid it next to him. Finally, he stood up. I felt the sweat beading on my back.

"Nice to meet you, sir," I said and shook his hand. He seemed friendly enough, but I couldn't read his expression.

Teresa introduced Steve to him next. Then he looked at us and asked, "So, what did you boys do today?"

I looked at Steve. We had agreed that we were going to deny everything and demand proof. Steve let me answer.

"Not a lot. Went to school. Got the car washed. I wanted it to look nice for your daughters. Just picked up Steve a little while ago."

"Did you notice anything when you walked up to the house tonight?" he asked.

I ignored my pride about the soft, white beauty that covered the hillside. "No, sir. Was there something we missed?" I ruffled my shirt to cool off.

"Well, our house got TP-ed this afternoon. Do you know anything about that?"

I tried to look surprised. Steve spoke up. "No, sir. It wasn't us, sir." I nodded my head.

"Are you sure? The boys I saw doing the TP-ing this afternoon looked an awful lot like the two of you. When I saw what they were doing, I went out to meet them. I'm pretty sure I surprised them. I brought my shotgun out with me. When they heard me cock it, they ran out of here faster than a rabbit running from a hound."

"I am sorry it wasn't the two of you," he went on. "I was going to thank you. It was one of the funniest things I've ever seen. I couldn't yell that I was only kidding, I was laughing so hard."

Only kidding? I couldn't believe it. If he was only kidding, then he wasn't going to shoot us this afternoon. And if he wasn't going to shoot us, then he wasn't mad. A huge wave of relief flooded over me.

I laughed with him. "Wow, that's pretty funny. I wonder who it was?"

I felt a little foolish. We must have looked pretty silly running down the hill. I still couldn't admit it was us, though. I was still scared that he'd get angry. Then he might stop Tanya from going to Sadie Hawkins with me.

I wasn't about to let that happen.

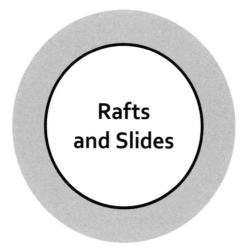

Rafts
and Slides

Rafting the whitewater rapids in the middle of the Austrian Alps was one of my favorite memories from Meg's and my first trip to Europe in 1989. When we returned twenty years later, I wanted to create a similar memory for our children, Sam and Chloe.

At the riverside, I shivered as I dipped my body into the water. The water was near freezing coming off the mountains. Fearless and a risk taker, I chose one of the front seats in the raft. In the midst of becoming a risk taker himself, Sam chose the other. I smiled at him, proud he was following in my footsteps, elated as I anticipated the upcoming ride. His eyes sparkled as he smiled back.

Before I had time to zip up my neoprene boots, eight of us, paddles in hand, and Pablo, our guide, were floating down the river. At the first set of rapids, I rowed hard, swallowed a liter of water, and felt the waves crash against me. When we exited the chute and I was still in my seat, I was excited and relieved. It was just like twenty years ago!

After we left the rapids, Pablo said it was time to jump out of the raft and float on the water. He would pick us up downriver. When everyone remained in their seat, with their eyes focused on the floor, I wondered when they had lost their sense of adventure. I looked over at Chloe with expectation in my eyes. She returned my look with her own, which suggested, "Let's do it." Chloe jumped in feet first. I brazenly flipped off backwards, somersaulting into the water.

Though I knew the water was freezing, I had forgotten how cold freezing actually was. When my body entered the water, it stole my breath away. I hurriedly surfaced, grabbed some air, and looked around to get my bearings. Chloe, I saw, was fine: floating lazily along, feet in front of her, a serene smile on her face. Then I saw the raft ten yards downriver. It was too far away. I began hyperventilating. I couldn't catch my breath. I would drown before they could pull me out of the water.

Pablo saw the terror on my face. He paddled as fast as he could toward me. He yelled at me to swim over. Sam pulled me back into the raft. After I was finally able to breathe, my fear began to dissipate. Chloe continued to float down the river without a care.

Before long, Chloe was back in the raft. She asked me if I was okay. I told her I was, though I knew that wasn't totally true. Before I could say anything else, we entered more rapids. With some sense of satisfaction, I maintained my role as leader in the front seat. I rowed hard, swallowed even more water, and no longer worried about getting thrown out of the raft after we survived several submergings. My stomach still churned from my earlier terror, however.

Later in the ride, Pablo offered us another opportunity to jump in the river. I watched as the others jumped overboard, splashed each other, and laughed heartily. The joy on their faces suggested exhilaration in their hearts. I stayed in the boat. The mere thought of jumping took my breath away. When we got back on dry land, I gladly accepted the schnapps I was offered. I asked for a double.

Riding a fiberglass sled down a mountain on a smooth cement track with a number of banked corners and flat straightaways seemed like a great way to recover my fearlessness and restore my sense of pride. Two days later, we headed for the alpine slide in Biberwier, Austria.

At the base of the mountain, we purchased seven tickets. Meg was only riding once. As we rode the chairlift up, I watched the sledders on the cement track below us. One group was bunched together, forming a traffic jam. The guy at the front looked like a turtle, he was going so slowly.

I hate traffic jams, especially on a ride, so I schemed to make sure it wouldn't happen to me. I assessed the speed of each of my family members. Sam, like me but younger and probably faster, should go first. I let Chloe follow Sam. I should have gone before her because I was fast like Sam, but I didn't want to hurt her feelings. I'd follow Chloe. Meg, our photographer at the top, would bring up the rear.

I announced the order, and we lined up to begin. With his picture taken, Sam got the green light and left. Chloe followed. My turn was next. After smiling for my picture, I prepared myself. I didn't want to catch Chloe and get stuck in a traffic jam, so when the green light flashed, I delayed my start—one one thousand, two one thousand, three one thousand. The attendant yelled something in German and motioned at me to go.

Pushing the stick forward I began my ride. Tentative at first, I pulled back on the stick to brake on the first curve. On the second curve I started to smile. You could develop a lot of speed on that sled. By the third turn I was flying. When the fourth turn came, I was traveling so fast I wondered how long it would be before I came up behind Chloe. "Look out, girl. Here I come!" I thought to myself.

I leaned into the next curve so I could fly even faster. All of a sudden, my rear end slipped off the sled. In the corner of my eye I watched the sled as it left the track. I remained behind in my shorts and T-shirt, continuing my flight down the cement. When I finally landed, I caught my breath and checked for damages. The track was fine. Not me, though. They weren't bleeding, but the newly formed raspberries on my left hand, my elbows, and my knees were beginning to burn. I also began to burn inside: *How could I have fallen off that sled?*

I had to put the flames out of my mind, though. Meg was coming. Careful to avoid touching anything red on my body, I got up, put my sled back on the track, sat down gingerly, and pushed the stick forward. I tried to get back up to flight speed but couldn't make myself. The scrape on my left hand made it difficult to push the stick forward, but mostly I was just plain afraid of crashing again.

Before long, I heard Meg close behind. That's when I realized I was that guy! I became the turtle. I caused a traffic jam. I hung my head. There was nothing I could do except meander slowly down. When I got to the bottom, Sam asked me why I took so long. I pointed out my elbows and knees. His face quickly morphed from frustration to concern. He gave me an "I'm sorry, Dad" as well as a "Bummer." It lessened the pain a little.

Three tickets still remained. I considered having Meg take the second run, but then I remembered the saying about falling off a horse. Despite the burning, I told Meg I was fine. Sam, Chloe, and I left for the chairlift.

As we headed toward the top of the mountain one more time, the bright sun assaulted my eyes. When I couldn't find my sunglasses, I knew they had flown off my face in the crash. I plotted to get them back. That mountain wasn't going to humiliate me and then steal my sunglasses, too.

At the top, there was no question I was going last. When the light turned green, I proceeded immediately, thoroughly scanning both sides of the track. At turn five, I saw my sunglasses on the left. I swiped as I passed, sure a restoration of pride was about to be awarded. When I looked in my hand for my prize, however, it was empty. My pride remained behind.

I rode the rest of the way down, disappointed but determined to get those sunglasses back. At the bottom, I purchased two tickets and asked Sam and Chloe to go back up. Seeing how much I wanted this, they were more than willing to help. After I laid out in exact detail where the sunglasses lay, Sam and Chloe left for the chairlift. I started to breathe a little easier. If anyone could retrieve them, it would be those two.

Twenty minutes later, Sam walked up to me. I thought he was teasing when he told me he couldn't find the sunglasses. I quickly realized he was serious when I saw no smile in his eyes or on his mouth. He apologized profusely for letting me down. I was in the middle of telling Sam it was really okay, that he didn't let me down, when Chloe walked up behind him. My eyes opened wide in disbelief when she showed me her hands and elbows. Each sported a raspberry, just like mine. She had fallen off her sled trying to recover my pride. She asked me if we could get some medicine to ease the burning. My own wounds began to sear.

With the day's adventure over, the four of us shuffled our way back to the car. As I drove to our bed and breakfast, the sun blazed in my eyes once more. Meg asked if I wanted her sunglasses. "Thanks but no thanks," I said. I flipped down the car visor and squinted.

A week later I told a friend about the memories I had created that week: terror in the water and crashing on the mountain. Then she asked me, "So, Brian, how is it getting old?" Tartly I replied, "I'm not getting old; I'm getting older!" I knew I had lost my fearlessness, my pride, my sunglasses, and a large portion of my hide on that mountain. But did she really have to remind me I was also losing my youth?

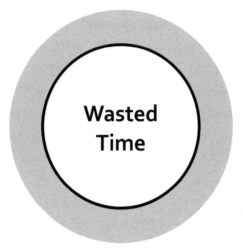

**Wasted
Time**

"**S**o how's the book coming, Brian?" Kate asked as we watched our daughters play field hockey.

"Good, but it keeps changing. Right now it's got three main ideas. Do you want to hear them?"

"Of course!" Kate said.

"The first idea is that even the most trying times have something of value for us. Second, we always seem to find a way through. Finally, talking about what's happening with close friends makes it easier."

Kate's face lit up. "Wow," she said. "Those are great. I'm sure there are lots of people who would love to hear you talk about that."

Kate's affirmation was music to my ears. I had been working on this project for over a year. Some days I was really excited about it. Other days, I worried that I was chasing my own tail. But Kate thought my ideas were interesting. Kate thought people would want to hear them. And Kate wasn't Judy, Joe, or Helen, my close friends who kept telling me to write. I couldn't stop smiling both inside and out.

On an errand after the game, I drove past a piece of property my friend Bob was developing. I called him up.

When he heard it was me, Bob took a deep breath. "Wow, it's nice to hear a friendly voice. It's been a long day."

"I just drove past the Isabella, Bob. The condos look great!"

"Thanks, but that project's going to keep me up tonight. Real estate's dipping. I'm not sure the condos will sell. I keep thinking I was foolish to invest so much. What really bugs me, though, is yesterday I couldn't stop thinking about how great things were going. How could it change so fast?"

Then he asked me. "Has this ever happened to you?"

I laughed. "All the time. I hate it. I just wish I could make it go away."

"Thanks," he said. His voice had relaxed.

I hung up, smiling. I wasn't worried about Bob. I knew he was talented and capable: he had been running a successful business for a long time. Even if the development flopped, somehow he would find a way through. I had seen it happen over and over again in my own life as well as in the lives of others.

Lying in bed that evening, I breathed a sigh of gratitude. Kate liked my ideas. I'd seen them at work on the phone with Bob. Everything was headed in the right direction. I fell into a sound sleep quickly.

The alarm startled me at 6 the next morning. Immediately, my heart raced, and my mind kicked into high gear. I was foolish to believe I could write a book. After all, even when I'd set aside writing time a few days earlier, nothing came out. I just sat there for two hours. Clearly, I wasn't supposed to be writing. I had wasted all that time I'd spent in front of the computer with a cup of coffee at my side. I hadn't spent enough time nurturing my therapy practice. It was sure to fall apart. I wouldn't be able to support my family.

A long, hot shower felt good but did nothing to alleviate my panic. A hug from Meg as I walked out the front door gave a momentary reprieve. Then I remembered that she would soon be moving out of the community she loved because we couldn't afford it any longer, because I had been wasting my time writing. My blood pressure skyrocketed.

On the way to work, I left a message for my friend Judy. When she called back, I recited the litany of my woes. I told her I had been wasting my time writing. I told her I had ruined my practice. I told her I needed to put my house up for sale. I could tell she wasn't experiencing the same panic. I must have not been making it clear enough, so I told her about my conversations with Kate and Bob.

"There's only one reason I could be on my last nerve after that great feedback. It's because I was completely misguided."

Judy's calm was palpable on the other end of the line. In fact, she seemed amused by what I was telling her. It was clear she still wasn't getting it. Now I was getting bugged.

"Well, you sure seem to be enjoying this."

"I like you like this," she replied.

"Excuse me?"

"I like you like this because I can relate to it. I know it well. It's just nice to know that you don't always have it together either."

"I'm really glad you like it. I hate it. I just wish it would go away."

"Of course you do, and it will. But I'm not worried about you."

In that moment, clarity returned. Judy wasn't worried about me. She knew I was talented and capable: I had been running a successful business for a long time. Even if the book flopped, she knew somehow I would find a way through. She had seen it happen over and over again in her own life as well as in the lives of others.

I started to laugh. Déjà vu. In the space of twelve hours, I had forgotten what I'd just spent a year writing about.

With a smile on my face, I dialed up Bob.

"Hello," he answered.

"Hey, Bob. This is Brian. You'll never guess what just happened to me."

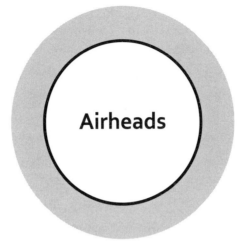

Airheads

One Saturday, my six-year-old son, Sam, asked if I could go to the store and buy some Airheads. Since I didn't know what Airheads looked like, I asked him to go with me. It was a win-win: Sam got the taffy he'd just seen advertised between his morning cartoons, and I got to spend time with him.

When we stopped at the local convenience store, Sam jumped out of the car and sprinted inside to find the candy aisle. There were so many flavors! Eventually he settled on five different kinds of Airheads, including the white-wrapper mystery flavor. As we drove home, Sam kept pulling the taffy out of his bag to read how each flavor was described.

Sitting at the kitchen table, Sam eagerly ripped open the wrapper with his little fingers. But instead of delight, I heard distress. "Oh no!" Sam cried out.

"What's up, Sam?"

"There's something wrong, Dad."

"What do you mean, 'there's something wrong'?"

"There's something wrong with the taffy."

I looked at the taffy in his hands. It looked fine to me. "I don't understand, Sam," I said.

"It's not bouncing around the room."

"What's not bouncing around the room?"

"The taffy, Dad. It's not bouncing around the room! In the commercial when they took the wrapper off, the taffy bounced all over the room. They said it was bouncing with flavor."

My heart sank as I realized what was happening.

"Sam, that's just part of the commercial. They make the taffy bounce around the room to convince you it tastes really good."

"So it's not going to bounce around the room?"

"No, Sam. I'm sorry."

Sam ingested this news and then bit into the taffy, the taffy that didn't bounce all over the room. His anticipation was gone, like the smile on his face. After he swallowed the last bite, his appetite was gone too. Part of me wanted to cry.

The other four pieces sat untouched on Sam's desk for a couple of weeks. One day my hunger got the better of me. I opened a piece. I think it was strawberry. The taffy didn't bounce around the room this time, either, but it tasted pretty good. When my last bite was gone, I wanted more.

As I opened a second piece, I thought about Sam. The commercial raised Sam's expectations so high, there was no way he could enjoy the taffy as it was. As a result, he lost out twice: once when the taffy didn't bounce around the room and once when he couldn't enjoy the actual taffy.

I wished I could protect him from being let down, from expecting one thing and getting another, yet I knew it would happen again. Life is that way. It doesn't always bounce around the room. I just hoped it didn't take him too long to figure out it still tastes pretty good.